ARCHITECTS &
MIMETIC RIVALRY

RENÉ GIRARD   LÉON KRIER   SAMIR YOUNÉS   KENT BLOOMER

To Anré

With friendship

Samir

ARCHITECTS &
MIMETIC RIVALRY

RENÉ GIRARD   LÉON KRIER   SAMIR YOUNÉS   KENT BLOOMER

Edited by
Samir Younés

(Cover Illustration: *Les rivalités architecturales,* Samir Younés, 2012.
Figures based on Giacinto Giminiani, *Des enfants en querelle,* 17th century.)

First published in Great Britain in 2012 by Papadakis Publisher

An imprint of New Architecture Group Limited

Kimber Studio
Winterbourne
Berkshire, RG20 8AN, UK
Tel. +44 (0) 1635 24 88 33
info@papadakis.net
www.papadakis.net

@papadakisbooks
PapadakisPublisher
PapadakisPublisher

Publishing Director: Alexandra Papadakis
Design Director: Aldo Sampieri
Editorial Assistants: Juliana Kassianos, Ian Caswell

ISBN 978 1 906506 33 9

A CIP catalogue record of this book is available from the British Library

Printed and bound in China

CONTENTS

Decapitated bust of Vitruvius, Viale di Villa Medici, Rome, Photo Samir Younés.

"Since men were of an imitative and teachable nature, they boasted of their inventions as they daily showed their various achievements in building, and thus, exercising their talents in rivalry, were rendered of better judgement daily."

Vitruvius II, 1, 3

INTRODUCTION
Architects, Imitation & Rivalry

Samir Younés

Architects accept their rivalries as inevitable accompaniments of their professional lives. Some explain these rivalries as collisions between opposing personalities, or as predictable outcomes of the deeply subjective ways in which architects pursue their self-expression. Others, of course, justify rivalries on the basis of ideological differences. Whereas these positions appropriately designate some of the causes and some of the effects of rivalries among architects, there is much in architectural rivalry that cannot be explained as the result of contesting comportments on the part of architects practising their self-centered expressions, or the clash between conflicting ideologies. In fact, these positions serve to unintentionally explain-away or ignore some of the psychological and pedagogical reasons for conflicts and antagonisms amongst architects.

As the following texts will show, a considerable part of architectural rivalry is paradoxically related to the ways in which architects learn their art. More specifically, their rivalries are related to mimesis or imitation, a phenomenon that is ontologically connected to the human character, a phenomenon that is an indispensable part of intellectual and emotional life. Imitation shapes our form-making capacities whether we seek to write a poem, compose a sonata, paint a portrait, or conceive a building. Imitation also helps to shape our personalities when we seek to model ourselves on the personality of an admired figure. As a paragon for learning, for adapting and contributing to society, imitation concerns forms and ideas, as well as the personalities that produced these forms and ideas. Whether we are poets, musicians, painters or architects, we mimetically appropriate forms and mimetically appropriate the personal traits of those who made these forms. Artistic identities are shaped by imitating preferred forms and by imitating the identities of their makers.

But although it is essential and useful, imitation has another side, one that makes it a cause for rivalry, and herein lies the paradox regarding imitation. As philosopher René Girard tirelessly explained, there is a peculiar side to rivalry that can be designated as *mimetic rivalry*.[i] Personal and ideological differences may be reasons for rivalry, but they are not necessarily reasons for *mimetic* rivalry. Mimetic rivalry occurs because of competition for what is commonly shared, for what is commonly desired. There is mimetic rivalry when the desire to imitate the other (a desire that is sometimes concealed) becomes desire to obtain the same forms, the same status. Either the common object, desired forms or status are shared, in which case there is no mimetic rivalry, or they are not shared, in which case desire becomes exacerbated and provokes conflicts or antagonisms. This engenders violence, mimetic violence, on intellectual, emotional, or even physical levels. As Girard explains in *A Theory by Which to Work: the Mimetic Mechanism*, this violence may continue based on the momentum of reciprocal reprisals until something or someone becomes the scapegoat whose sacrifice neutralizes the antagonisms – at least temporarily. And one of the important traits of the scapegoat is that it is always innocent of the reasons that caused the antagonism in the first place. Ornament for example, as Kent Bloomer argues in his essay: "The Sacrifice of Ornament in the Twentieth Century", became one such a sacrificial scapegoat due to the terrible antagonism waged by the protagonists of modernist architecture against the protagonists of traditional architecture.

Girardian mimetic rivalry suggests that the conflict may have begun because of the desire to possess the same forms, but this desire is mediated by someone who serves as a model. Our desire for objects, according to Girard, is based less on the object and more on another person's desire, another person's mediation, a person whom we consider to be a model for our actions. The less a would-be imitator and a would-be model have in common, the less likely is their mimetic rivalry. There is no possible mimetic rivalry between Don Quixote and Sancho Panza because they do not desire the same things.

Since 2004, based on Girard's work, Léon Krier and Samir Younés had been exchanging views about the many motivations for the terrible rivalries between architects. The commonly accepted reasons such as professional jealousies (what Immanuel Kant termed "envious competitive vanity") or ideological differences were insufficient to explain why some aspects of architectural rivalries were concealed or suppressed, while other aspects remained openly exposed. There were still rivalries between architects who are professionally quite prosperous, and there were still rivalries between architects who shared the same beliefs, the same architectural forms and theory. Krier and Younés saw the full applicability of Girard's concept of mimetic rivalry to the rivaling psychology of architects, for it explained the architects' double mimetic relation to their forms and to their personae. It explained the link between the ways in which architects appropriate the forms that they use in their compositions (formal imitation), and

Nanni di Banco, Quattro Santi Coronati, early fifteenth century, detail, Orsanmichele, Florence. Photo Samir Younés.

the ways in which they consider a highly esteemed figure as a direct model (personal imitation).

Many architects conceive of their identities, and differences, as an amalgamation of formal and personal identities. This amalgamation is at the basis of their mimetic rivalries as S. Younés maintains in his essay: "The Other Side of Imitation". Moreover, many architects conflate the notion of artistic identity with that of artistic uniqueness. Under the immense influence of cultural modernism, they consider themselves the creators of forms *ex nihilo*. They wish to develop unique identities, and they come to see these identities in a potently exclusive way. In other words, they understand and affirm identity as difference. This affirmation makes them overlook the fact that to have identity implies at once what is unique and what is in common in cultural production. "Our own identity is but the intersection of all that makes us identical to innumerable others"[ii] reminded R. Girard. Identity is mediated by imitation, by the rational appropriation and transformation of intelligible universals; in other words, by the judicious use of tradition for the practical uses of reason in architecture.

In the social sciences, imitation is a well-recognized, well-studied human trait, but it is less so amongst architects. Contemporary architects may concede that imitation played a role in the past, but they allow little space for this concept when it comes to their contemporary practice. Consequently, their understanding of imitation, whether in its beneficial side (mimesis of form) or its deleterious side (mimetic rivalry), is hindered precisely by the lack of recognition of the ways in which imitation operates. Prior to the advent of modernist thought, imitation and invention were considered to be two facets of the same coin. Imitation meant that objects are made out of combinations of other objects, cities and buildings out of combinations of other cities and buildings. In its best aspects, invention sought to improve the rational choice from exemplary precedents without losing from sight the nature, ends and means of each art. With modernism invention became an end in itself. The two different facets of the coin: imitation and invention, now became two identical facets: invention and invention. Artistic and architectural production was now considered to be *all invention*; or so was the prevalent claim. Imitation and invention came to be considered as antagonistic rather than complementary concepts. To be inventive meant that artists and architects practised *creatio ex nihilo*, the making of objects out of nothing. Consequently, architects who have been educated in the tenets of modernism refuse to acknowledge the concept of imitation even though they learn and appropriate their preferred architectural forms through undeniably imitative acts. They wish to be unique and produce the unseen, even if their artistic and personal identities are inextricably connected to the artistic and personal identities of others. As a result, they hide their imitative inclinations as L. Krier poignantly explains in: "Imitation, Hidden or Declared". The psychological act of hiding imitative inclinations bears a strong relation to the desire to conceal the influences of others, and an even stronger desire to veil an undeclared mimetic rivalry.

Girard's pessimism, a well-founded pessimism based on insightful observations of mimetic rivalry in inter-personal relations (as well as inter-group and inter-national relations), leads him to believe that mimetic rivalry is inescapably linked to human comportment. Its patterns can only be broken by some form of scapegoating. Might there be a set of measures capable of alleviating such a form of violence? Even if conflicts and antagonisms will not go away, and even if architects' political lives provide for ample

exchanges of mimetic rivalry, might the architect's special relationship to the city and to tradition offer some form of psychological temperance? Might psychologist James Hillman's assertion that "tradition has in itself a civilizing effect", and his appeal to the wise and disciplined clemency of the Senex, which tradition at its best inherently contains, hold the hope for a psychology of moderation? Might the civilizing value of tradition remind architects of their exceptional relationship to the City? For they participate at once in building the city's intellectual edifice as well as ideating the city's physical edifices.

Many architects build *in the city*, but fewer architects build *the City*. All architects, however, are called to build the City's public and private realms; and this project is greatly enhanced when architects work toward a good that is larger than their own. This is not to say that for architecture to be successful, all professional conflicts must be suspended. Quite the contrary, the architectural endeavor is frequently the result, or rather the resultant, of many conflicting claims (the aims of patrons, the will of builders, the insertion of a new building that qualitatively transforms an existing context) which could be successfully brought together in a synthesis that transcends them all. Contrary to antagonism, the terms of a conflict do not necessarily eliminate each other. Out of conflict useful results can emerge.

In their highest aspects, politics (the art of living together justly) and architecture (the art of building beautiful, enduring, and commodious shelter for public and private needs) undertake to reciprocally perfect the ethical and physical enclosure of the City. Many exemplary urban and architectural forms resulted from such fortunate historical moments which were not devoid of conflicts between the aims of politics and the expressions of architectural character. This has nothing to do with inflicting political content or ideology onto architectural character – the lessons of the past century have demonstrated the foolishness of such associations – only to underline that one of architecture's main purposes resides in endowing the buildings of the *polis* with their proper character (e.g. religious, institutional, mercantile, residential). Reciprocal influence between politics and architecture has little to do with utopian thought in the sense of unrealistic, saccharine, or ill-defined visions for an unrealizable city based on inaccessible ideals. But rather in the sense of tradition, the collection of reasoned practices that builds the *ev topos*, the well-place, the Good City, the *città felice*. Must the Good City always remain locked inside the gilded binding of hopeful treatises of architecture?

Following the failures of several utopian projects, many contemporary architects understandably recoil from entertaining utopian thought. And yet they still, deep down, consider what architecture presently *is* and imaginatively, or imagistically construct what it *could* or *ought* to be – with good and bad results. But flanking these good intentions, the psychological relations between architects is a world brimming-over with rivalries, with long-lasting antagonisms. And these rivalries concern more than ideological differences regarding architectural form. They are also mimetic rivalries – rivalries about that which is commonly held. The result is that rivalry is a fairly diffused phenomenon among architects, amalgamated as it is with their understanding of identity and otherness, reputation and ambition, authority and exhibitionism.

City-making and the psychologies of those who make cities are closely linked. It is not the purpose of this book to present strategies for reforming the City and reforming the rivaling psychologies of architects who build it. These are the pursuits of more ambitious and lengthy studies. It is, however, the aim of this book to draw attention to the destabilizing influence of mimetic rivalry on the psychology of those who build cities and the aesthetic culture of cities; and this role is all the more destabilizing because it remains largely unrecognized.

i. René Girard's concepts of mimetic desire and mimetic rivalry were developed in a long list of publications spanning over five decades. His works include: *Mensonge romantique et vérité romanesque*, Grasset, 1961, English translation: *Deceit, Desire and the Novel: Self and Other in Literary Structure*, Baltimore, Johns Hopkins University Press, 1966; *La violence et le sacré*, Grasset, 1973, English translation: *Violence and the Sacred*, Translated by Patrick Gregory, Baltimore, Johns Hopkins University Press, 1977; *Des choses cachées depuis la fondation du monde*, Grasset, 1978, English translation: *Things Hidden since the Foundation of the World: Research undertaken in collaboration with J.-M. Oughourlian and G. Lefort*, Stanford University Press, 1987; *To Double Business Bound: Essays on Literature, Mimesis, and Anthropology*, Baltimore, Johns Hopkins University Press, 1978; *Le bouc émissaire*, Grasset, 1982, English translation: *The Scapegoat*, Baltimore, Johns Hopkins University Press, 1986;

Quand ces choses commenceront, 1994; *The Girard Reader*, James G. Williams Ed., New York: Crossroad, 1996; *Celui par qui le scandale arrive*, Pluriel, 2001; *La voix méconnue du réel*, Livre de poche, 2002; *Oedipus Unbound: Selected Writings on Rivalry and Desire*, Mark R. Anspach, Ed., Stanford University Press, 2004; *Les origines de la culture*, Pluriel, 2004, English translation: *Evolution and Conversion: Dialogues on the Origins of Culture*, London, Continuum, 2008; *Achever Clausewitz*, Carnets Nord, 2007; *Mimesis and Theory: Essays on Literature and Criticism, 1953-2005*, Robert Doran Ed., Stanford University Press, 2008; *Anoréxie et désir mimétique*, L'Herne, 2008. Girard was elected to the Académie française in 2005.

ii. René Girard, "Les appartenances." in *Politiques de Cain*, Domenica Mazzù Ed., Desclée de Bouwer, Paris, 2004, p. 20.

Here, then, I had at last got a

theory by which to work.

Charles Darwin, *Autobiography*

'A Theory by Which to Work':
The Mimetic Mechanism

René Girard

1. THE MIMETIC MECHANISM AT WORK

You have always put forward a genetic explanation of the origin of culture alongside a hypothesis of its historical evolution. In this chapter for the sake of clarity, we would like to discuss the core notions of your theory in a synchronic form, as a mechanism which engenders both inter-individual psychological dynamics and more general social phenomena. And to start with, we would like you to distinguish between the notion of mimetic desire and mimetic mechanism as set out in your books.

The expression 'mimetic mechanism' covers a phenomenological sequence which is quite broad. It describes the whole process beginning with mimetic desire, which then becomes mimetic rivalry, eventually escalating to the stage of a mimetic crisis, finally ending with the scapegoat resolution. In order to account for this sequence, we should start from the very beginning, i.e. with mimetic desire. First of all, we should distinguish between desire and appetites. Appetites for things like food or sex – which aren't necessarily connected with desire – are biologically grounded. However, all appetites can be contaminated with mimetic desire as soon as there is a model, and the presence of the model is the decisive element in my theory. If desire is mimetic, i.e. imitative, then the subject will desire the same object possessed or desired by his model. Now, either the subject is in the same relational domain as his model or he is in a different one. If he is in a different domain, of course he cannot possess his model's object and he can have what I call a relationship of external mediation with his model. For instance, if he and his favourite movie star, who might act as his role-model, live in different worlds, then a direct conflict between subject and model is out of the question, and the mediation

The Death of Abel. Illustration from Doré's *The Holy Bible*, engraved by Pisan, 1866,
Gustave Doré/ Private Collection / Ken Welsh / The Bridgeman Art Library.

ends up being a positive one – or at least not a conflictual one. However, if he belongs to the same contextual domain, to the same world as his model, if his model is also his peer then his model's objects are accessible. Therefore, rivalry eventually erupts. I call this type of mimetic relationship *internal mediation*, and it is intrinsically self-reinforcing. Due to the physical and psychological proximity of subject and model, the mediation tends to become more and more symmetrical: the subject will tend to imitate his model as much as his model him. Eventually, the subject will become the model of his model just as the imitator will become the imitator of his imitator. One is always moving towards more symmetry, and thus always towards more conflict, for symmetry cannot but produce doubles, as I call them at this moment of intense rivalry.[ii] Doubling occurs as soon as the object has disappeared in the heat of the rivalry: the two rivals become more and more concerned with defeating the opponent for the sake of it, rather than obtaining the object, which eventually becomes irrelevant, as it only exists as an excuse for the escalation of the dispute. Thus, the rivals become more and more undifferentiated, identical: doubles. A mimetic crisis is always a crisis of undifferentiation that erupts when the roles of subject and model are reduced to that of rivals. It's the disappearance of the object which makes it possible. This crisis not only escalates between the contenders, but it becomes contagious with bystanders.

This hypothesis contradicts the modern conception of desire, seen as the authentic expression of the self. Desire is not something which 'belongs' to the individual, but it is rather a form of direction of appetites and interests, as it provides an augmentation of cognitive focalization in respect of the objects of reality, and this 'vector' of direction is provided by a model.

The real question is: what is desire? The modern world is arch-individualistic. It wants desire to be strictly individual, unique. In other words, the attachment to the object of desire is, in a way, predetermined. If desire is only mine, I will always desire the same things. If desire is so fixed, it means that there isn't much difference between desire and instincts. In order to have *mobility* of desire – in relation to both appetites and instincts from one side and the social milieu from the other – the relevant difference is *imitation*, that is, the presence of the *model* or models, since everybody has one or more. Only mimetic desire can be *free*, can be *genuine* desire, human desire, because it *must* choose a model more than the object itself. Mimetic desire is what makes us human, what makes it possible for us to breakout from routinely animalistic appetites, and construct our own, albeit inevitably unstable, identities. It is this very mobility of desire, its mimetic nature, and this very instability of our identities, that makes us capable of *adaptation*, that gives us the possibility to learn and to *evolve*.

It is interesting what you say because if one considers pathologies such as autism, which is defined as a radical impairment in the relational activity with others, what has become clear to researchers is the fact that imitation is the mechanism by which the infant comes to know something of the inner life of the other. It provides the early bridge between self and the other. The infant's capacity to translate the behaviour of others and to perform the same behaviour is foundational for its later development in intersubjectivity, communication and social cognition.[iii] *Failing to imitate means radical cultural impairment.*

Perhaps we fail to understand the mimetic nature of desire because we rarely refer to the first stages of human development. Every child has appetites, instincts and a given cultural milieu in which he learns by imitating adults or peers. Imitation and learning are inseparable. Normally the word 'imitation' is reserved to designate what is considered inauthentic – and maybe that's why in the humanities there isn't a real theory of psychological action that accounts for imitative behaviour. In discussing the mimetic hypotheses Paul Ricoeur said that if you are affected by imitative behaviour you are seen as a child who plays, meaning you are not in control of your actions – and in fact in imitation there is always a certain degree of 'unconsciousness' involved.[iv] What we have in the social sciences are normally theories, as for instance in Piaget, which account for these phenomena and behaviours limited to the early stages of psychological personal development, and they are seldom extended to the lives of adults. We don't resign ourselves to the recognition that we are imitating people we admire and envy as the expression of our desires. We see it as something to be ashamed of. Given this lack of understanding of mimesis, one may wonder if it wouldn't be better to return to imitation in the terms posited by Greek philosophy, as for instance by Plato or Aristotle. When Plato talks about imitation in the *Republic*, suddenly the image of the mirror appears, as one of the signs of the mimetic crisis: it is the sign of the appearance of the doubles, and that's why Plato eventually refuses mimesis, because he knows the danger of conflict behind imitative ideas and practices, which are not simply related to art, but to human affairs in general.[v]

Why have you opted for the word mimetic *instead of* imitative?

I employ the two words differently. There is less awareness in *mimetism* and more in *imitation*. I do not want to reduce mimesis to mimetic desire in all its forms. It is a typical twentieth century epistemological attitude. Behaviourism, for instance, is a total refusal of imitation. This is also the case with Freud – as I already remarked in *Violence and the Sacred*.[vi] In *Beyond the Pleasure Principle*, the word *imitation* (*Nachahmung*) is everywhere, but it has no role in Freud's theory. I think one of the reasons for this general avoidance is that the concept of imitation, removed from its conflictual element, is too 'simple' and disappoints the present (very mimetic) appetite for 'complexity'. I'm fully aware of this because my first book exemplified this way of thinking. This attitude of refusing to discuss the concept of imitation is still a dominant trend in our culture, and probably the emergence of mimetic theory is part of this process, but also a reaction to it. In his book *Le Feu sacré*, Régis Debray 'praises' me in 15 ferocious pages; he ties my work to Tarde's and to the tradition of imitation starting from Aristotle. Of course, he never takes into consideration the notion of mimetic rivalry…

As a matter of fact, in recent years imitation has become a topic of growing interest within the fields of cognitive science and neuroscience.[vii] *Developmental psychologists have claimed that newborns imitate in a way that cannot be explained in terms of conditioning or the triggering of innate behaviours.*[viii] *Neurophysiologists have discovered an interesting class of neuron, the so-called 'mirror neurons', which 'fire' both when an individual is performing a particular movement, and when observing the same movement by another person.*[ix]

Indeed, this is a very promising development in the understanding of the deep cognitive structure of our mimetic behaviour, and Michel Serres is very interested in this connection.[x] However, if you survey this literature, you will soon realize that acquisition and appropriation are *never* included among the mode of behaviours that are likely to be imitated. Theories of imitation never speak about acquisitive imitation and mimetic rivalry. And this is the crucial point of the mimetic theory. Mimetic rivalry becomes evident if we consider interactions among children. A child

has a relationship of external mediation, meaning positive imitation, with adults, and of internal mediation, that is, imitation and rivalry with his peers. It is a matter not so much of experimental psychology, but of everyday observation. The first thinker who marvelously defined this type of mimetic rivalry was St. Augustine, in his *Confessions*. Augustine describes two infants who have the same 'wet nurse'. Even if there is more than enough milk for both, the two children are rivals for the milk. They want to have it all in order to prevent the other from having any.[xi] Even though this example is mythical, it symbolizes very well the role of the mimetic rivalry, not only among infants but also within humanity in general. Mimetic conflicts are evident in children as well as in adults, although we always refuse to acknowledge that our actions are affected by this form of behaviour.

2. MIMETIC RIVALRY

Although the mobility of the desire is a distinctive feature of the historical process of the emergence of the modern individual, which accelerated after the Renaissance, you state that mimetic desire isn't a modern invention.

No, it isn't a modern invention. What is distinctive in modern times is that the array of models to choose from is much larger and there are no longer class differences in terms of desire – meaning that any external mediation in modern society has collapsed. People at the lowest social level desire what people at the highest level have.[xii] They think they should have it, whereas in historical periods social stratification and division was much more rigid (think of the slaves in ancient Greece or the caste system in India) and access to specific goods and items was very limited or strictly regimented and controlled by social and economic class.

Nonetheless, mimetic desire and mimetic rivalry were present and clearly defined in myth and in religious scriptures, as for instance in the Bible or in the Indian Vedas. The most interesting texts from my viewpoints are the Brahmanas, which are compilations of rites and commentaries on sacrifice. From a descriptive standpoint they are wonderful texts to illustrate what I call mimetic rivalry.[xiii] Of course, we have to assume (as I always do) that in myths there is an element of referentiality, and they are not pure invention of naive minds, as people normally believe. Myths are forms of organization of knowledge – and in fact the word Veda means *knowledge*, science – and this knowledge is essentially related to desire and sacrifice.

In I See Satan Fall Like Lightning,[xiv] *you also claimed that the mimetic desire and rivalry is evident in the Bible, which moves from a purely descriptive to a more normative understanding of imitation and conflict.*

Yes. Starting from Genesis, desire is clearly represented as mimetic: Eve is induced to eat the apple by a snake, and Adam mimetically desires the same object through Eve, in a clear chain of imitation. There is also an element of envy in the killing of Abel by Cain, and *envy* is one of the commonest names given to mimetic rivalry. Then I attach a great importance to the last commandment of the Decalogue: 'You shall not covet your neighbour's house. You shall not covet your neighbour's wife, or his manservant or maidservant, his ox or donkey, or anything that belongs to your neighbour' (Exodus 20.17).[xv] Here you have a clear definition of mimetic desire, because the law tries to enumerate in a long list all the objects that shouldn't be desired. Then the law realizes in mid-course that there isn't any point in listing all these numerous objects: the fixed point is the neighbour and everything that belongs to him. The tenth commandment finally prohibits 'everything that belongs to your neighbour'. This commandment is a prohibition of mimetic desire. But what comes before the tenth commandment? 'You shall not murder. You shall not commit adultery. You shall not steal. You shall not give false testimony against your neighbour' (Exodus 20.13-16). So, these four are all crimes against the neighbour: killing him, stealing his wife, stealing his properties and slandering him. Where do they all come from? The fifth commandment asks the question and discovers the cause: mimetic desire. The last words – 'everything that belongs to the neighbour' – put the neighbour first, as the model. Thus the notion of mimetic desire is already present in the Old Testament.

The Gospels talk in terms of imitation and not in terms of prohibition, but what is at stake is the same principle already present in the tenth commandment. Most people wrongly assume that in the Gospels imitation is limited solely to one model, the imitation of Jesus, which is proposed in a non-mimetic context. But it isn't true. We are always within the context suggested by the tenth commandment. Jesus asks us to imitate him, rather than the neighbour, in order to protect us from the mimetic rivalry. The model that encourages mimetic rivalry isn't necessarily worse than we are, he is maybe much better, but he desires in the same way we do, selfishly, avidly; therefore we imitate his selfishness, and he is a bad model for us, just as we will be a bad model for him in the process of doubling that is bound to take place as soon as the rivalry escalates.

3. SCAPEGOATING AND SOCIAL ORDER

The phenomenology of the mimetic desire as illustrated seems mostly related to inter-individual relationships; however, as you have explained in your books, it can also have a disruptive effect on a larger scale, producing mimetic crises and destroying the social order.

Indeed. While the mimetic machine of this reciprocal imitation of rivals, of this 'double business', is in operation, it stores up conflictual energy and, of course, it tends to spread in all directions because, as it continues, the mechanism only becomes more mimetically attractive to bystanders – if two persons are fighting over the same object, then this object seems more valuable to bystanders. Therefore, it tends to attract more and more people, and as it does so, its mimetic attractiveness keeps increasing. While this happens, there is also a tendency for the object to disappear, to be destroyed in the conflict. As I said before, for the mimesis to become purely antagonistic the object has to disappear. When this happens, the proliferation of doubles occurs, and with it the mimetic crisis is bound to take place. As antagonism and violence erupt, they both spread in the same mimetic way, by cumulative resentment and vengeance, producing a state of Hobbesian radical crisis of all against all.

The most (or rather the only) effective form of reconciliation – that would stop this crisis, and save the community from total self-destruction – is the convergence of all collective anger and rage toward a random victim, a scapegoat, designated by mimetism itself, and unanimously adopted as such. In the frenzy of the mimetic violence of the mob, a focal point suddenly appears in the shape of the 'culprit' who is thought to be the cause of the disorder and the one who brought the crisis into the community. He is singled out and unanimously killed by the community. He isn't any guiltier than any other, but the whole community strongly believes he is. The killing of the scapegoat ends the crisis, since the transference against it is unanimous. That is the importance of the scapegoat mechanism: it channels the collective violence against one arbitrarily chosen member of the community, and this victim becomes the common enemy of the entire community, which is reconciled as a result.

The mimetic nature of this process is particularly obvious in rituals, where all these stages of development are re-enacted. Why does the ritual so often begin with concocted disorder, with a deliberate simulated cultural crisis, and end with a victim who is expelled or ritually killed? The purpose is simply to re-enact the mimetic crisis which leads to the scapegoat mechanism. The hope is that the re-enactment of this mechanism will reactivate its power of reconciliation.

Do you think perhaps that the passage from the mimesis of acquisition and the escalation of doubles up to the victimary resolution is not as strictly consequential as your explanation would suggest? Crisis could be provoked by circumstances which are not necessarily linked to the acquisitive mimesis, as for instance in the case of episodes of actual plague. A scapegoat may be sought and found because of ignorance of the biological basis of the disease, and the need to find someone 'responsible' for the crisis. Therefore we should try to separate the phenomenology of mimetic desire and mimetic rivalry from the scapegoat mechanism itself.

The crisis could indeed be rooted in an objective catastrophic event: an epidemic, a famine, a flood. But this objective event develops into a mimetic crisis which, as explained, very likely ends in scapegoating. There would be no scapegoat if the community didn't shift from mimesis of the desired object, which divides to a mimesis of antagonism, which permits all alliances against the victim. The whole mechanism is contained in that shift. What is crucial for the resolution of this crisis is the shift from the desire of the object, which divides the imitators, to the hatred of the rival, which reconciles when hatred is channeled onto a single victim. The rivalrous and conflictual mimesis is spontaneously and automatically transformed into reconciliatory mimesis. For, if it is impossible for the rivals to find an agreement around the object which everybody wants, this very agreement is quickly found, on the contrary, against the victim whom everybody hates.

To summarize, then: the victimary mimetic is triggered when mimetic desire turns into mimetic rivalry. This rivalry, this mimetic conflict, through mechanisms of social contagion, reaches social proportions, and ultimately a scapegoat polarization and resolution, with a final mimetic reconciliation of the community.

That is correct. In the beginning the mimetic rivalries may be separated centres of attention, but then they tend to contaminate each other more and more, becoming more mimetically attractive as they include more rivals, since mimesis is cumulative. By its dynamics, the scapegoat mechanism must ultimately end with one *skandalon* devouring all the others, and therefore it produces one single victim. If there is one single victim, once the victim is killed, there isn't any rebound of vengeance, because everybody is hostile to this one victim. Thus, there is at least one moment in which peace is restored within the community, and the community never praises itself for this reconciliation; it regards this new acquisition of order as a gift from the victim it just killed. This is both malefic because it caused the crisis, but also beneficial because its death restored peace, and therefore the scapegoat becomes divinized in the archaic sense, that is, the all-powerful, Almighty both for good and for bad simultaneously. So it is a purely mechanical fact, although it isn't deterministic. It is possible to say why this or that victim is selected in different scapegoat events, but they do not add up to a single general rule.

Could you clarify the difference between a mechanical and a deterministic fact?

The mimetic mechanism isn't deterministic because from one side there is an element of randomness in the selection of the scapegoat victim; from the other it doesn't follow that every single social group involved in a mimetic crisis will necessarily find the scapegoat mechanism resolution.[xvi] Indeed, this is a crucial point. I have never said that the mimetic mechanism is deterministic. We can hypothetically assume that several prehistoric groups did not survive precisely because they didn't find a way to cope with the mimetic crisis; their mimetic rivalries didn't find a victim who polarized their rage, saving them from self-destruction. We could even conceive of groups that solved one or two crises through the founding murder but failed to re-enact it ritually, developing a durable religious system, and therefore succumbing to the next crisis. What I have said is that the threshold of culture is related to the scapegoat mechanism, and that the first known institutions are closely related to its deliberate and planned re-enactment.

Could you then say that the victim has to be randomly chosen?

Not necessarily. It depends on the degree of awareness of the scapegoaters, but also of the victim. For instance, if someone denounces the scapegoat mechanism, and if the scapegoat mechanism eventually prevails, the scapegoat mechanism is immediately provided with its victim, which is that particular troublemaker. This works in the case of the Servant of Jahweh, and in the case of Christ. Therefore I don't make Jesus a random victim, contrary to what Hans Urs von Balthazar argues in *La Gloire et la Croix*. Christ flags himself as the victim to his persecutors. This pattern works also in the case of Plato – which shows how aware Plato was of this mechanism. There is an astonishing sentence in Plato, which still remains unexplained. One of the characters in the *Republic* says that if there existed a perfect man in whom there would be absolutely no evil, no vengeance, he would end up being killed.[xvii] Socrates is close to being such a man. He criticizes cultural inequities; therefore, he designates himself as a scapegoat. This could perhaps be derived from the Bible, which Plato may have known, since he travelled to Egypt, where there were many Jews at that time.[xviii] However, there isn't a real history of the Diaspora and the early period is still mysterious. Nietzsche wrote about the fact that Plato knew the Bible. (Maybe that is why he did not like Plato…)[xix]

Going back to your question: I do not think we could say that the victim is randomly chosen. After all, randomness means pure chance. If we look at myths, we will see that the victims are too often chosen among physically challenged people or foreigners, to be a purely random event: these 'preferential signs' increase the possibilities of being selected as scapegoat. It is very clear in Isaiah, in the 'Servant of Jahweh'. People have what could be called a natural dislike for exceptions, physical deformities, which become signs of victimizations. In the 'Servant of Jahweh', there is a passage that reads: 'He had no beauty or majesty to attract us to him, nothing in his appearance that we should desire him. He was despised and rejected by men, a man of sorrows, and familiar with suffering. Like one from whom men hide their faces he was despised, and we esteemed him not' (Isaiah 53.2-3). Preferential signs of victimization are given as *reasons* for victimizing this person, reasons that are insufficient, scandalous, but do not allow us to always speak of pure randomness. Infirmities, or unpleasant traits, are mistaken for guilt. That is the reason why in medieval illustrations witches very often are represented a little bit like the Jews in anti-Semitic caricatures, with distorted features, hunchbacked, limping. If you look at the Greek gods, far from being beautiful, they are very often like that: short, one-eyed, mutilated, stuttering, deformed (there is a parodical text by Lucian of Samosata, *Tragodopodagra*, which is all about that).[xx] There are also exceptions, which show out-of-the-ordinary beauty, like that of Apollo or Venus, but we have to remember that both extremes are usually more scapegoated than average people. The king is a preferred target for victimization. After all, the institution itself originates in scapegoating. Therefore, the king tends to go back to his original status.[xxi] So we shouldn't say randomness *stricto sensu*, and it would be better to say arbitrariness.

Therefore, it is a combination of arbitrariness and necessity.

Very often, but not necessarily, because even if there isn't a preferential sign of victimization, the scapegoat will be chosen anyway. At that crucial moment something will often be interpreted as a sign. Anything. And everybody thinks that they have found the solution, the culprit. In a way, the scapegoat mechanism functions like false science, like a great discovery that is made, or something that is suddenly revealed, and then one reads in the eyes of other people the same insight, that, therefore, the conviction of the crowd becomes increasingly reinforced. Hocart talks about a sort of naïve 'fetishism' of the physical object seen as direct evidence.[xxii] Take the example of Phaedra, the protagonist of Euripides' tragedy *Hippolytus*, who kills herself blaming her stepson.

Why is Theseus easily convinced that Hippolytus raped her? Because Phaedra has his sword. In the biblical story of Joseph, Potiphar's wife has Joseph's tunic, which seems to prove that the young man tried to have sexual relations with her. There is a physical object that looks like a proof, evidence, exhibit No. 1, so to speak.

With reference to randomness, nonetheless, as you said in Things Hidden, *rituals seem to keep 'memory' of the aleatory elements at the base of victim selection in the scapegoat mechanism, by staging games or riddles, for contingent selection of the victim to be sacrificed.*[xxiii] *At least the selection of the surrogate victim could be made by pure chance.*

That's true. That was also related to my reading of Caillois' book *Les Jeux et les hommes*, in which it is evident that the only element in playing and games which is not shared with animals is in fact *alea*, chance, which is a cultural byproduct of ritual practice.[xxiv] Of course the outcome of a chance game could be double: either you are selected as a victim, or your life is spared. Ritual is a cultural form that prepares for the sacrificial resolution, but it serves mainly as a form of controlling violence, and the increasing sophistication of ritualistic forms and elements helps in distancing further and further a given culture from the original violence implicit in the ritualistic act. That's evident in several myths. By solving the riddle of the Sphinx, Oedipus, as a sacrificial victim, saves himself and the city of Thebes, which enthrones him as its king. The labyrinth is a ritual architectural machine which has the Minotaur (i.e. sacrificial violence) at its centre. If one 'solves' it, as in the case of Theseus with the help of Ariadne, he can spare his life, becoming a hero. All these performative elements are also common in the so-called 'rites of passage'.[xxv]

In order to account for the escalation involved in the scapegoat mechanism, could we say that it presupposes the previous collectivization of the phenomenon of the doubles as seen on the individual scale, which leads to the collective undifferentiation, which then involves the entire social group? Undifferentiation is the mirroring of the mechanism of doubling at the social level.

Yes. The less differentiated people become, the easier it is to decide that any one of them is guilty. The word *doubles* is the very symbol of desymbolization, and it means undifferentiation: the absence of all differences. The mythical twins are a metaphor of undifferentiation. The twins played a great role in my discovery of the scapegoat mechanism. I remember when I was reading Lévi-Strauss, that in his theory everything is difference up to the point that there is difference even between twins. But the twins are a logical denial of difference, and Lévi-Strauss doesn't take that into account. Lévi-Strauss, following Saussure, says that language cannot express any absence of difference. However, language does talk about undifferentiation. This is what twins are for, and the metaphor is taken with deadly seriousness by certain societies in which twins are actually killed.

(Of course, other societies are aware that biological twins haven't anything to do with the process of social undifferentiation, and nothing happens in these cases.) That was very important in my critique of Lévi-Strauss. Nonetheless, Lévi-Strauss is indispensable for the discovery of what twins really mean. In order to fear twins, there must be the primacy of difference. Primitive culture can talk about undifferentiation, even if in principle language cannot. Language resorts to twins in order to talk about undifferentiation. Language is wiser than Lévi-Strauss realizes, more realistic.

It is because the scapegoat mechanism actually precedes any sort of cultural order, and in particular it precedes language. Indeed, it is what allows culture to be developed.

Yes. The question, then, is how does culture develop? The answer is through ritual. As I said, in an effort to prevent frequent and unpredictable episodes of mimetic violence, acts of planned, controlled, mediated, periodical, ritualized surrogate violence were put in place. Ritual in this way becomes like a school because it repeats the same scapegoat mechanism over and over again on substitute victims. And since ritual is the resolution of a crisis, it always intervenes at points of crisis; it will always be there at the same point of the mimetic crisis. Therefore, ritual will turn into the institution that regulates any sort of crisis, like the crisis of adolescence and the rites of passage, like the crisis of death, which generates funeral rituals, like the crisis of disease, which

generates ritual medicine. Whether the crisis is real or imaginary makes very little difference, because an imaginary crisis may cause a real catastrophe.

There are two possible views of ritual. On the one hand, the Enlightenment view for which religion is superstition and if ritual is everywhere it's because cunning and avid priests impose their abracadabras on the good people. On the other hand, if we simply consider that the clergy cannot really precede the invention of culture, then religion must come first and far from being a derisory farce, it appears as the origin of the whole culture. And humanity is the child of religion.

Hocart supports this claim by writing the following:

Ritual isn't in good odour with our intellectuals. It is associated in their minds with a clerical movement for which most of them nurse an antipathy. They are therefore unwilling to believe that institutions which they approve of, and which seem to them so eminently practical and sensible as modern administration, should have developed out of the hocus-pocus which they deem ritual to be. In their eyes only economic interests can create anything as solid as the state. Yet if they would only look about them they would everywhere see communities banded together by interest in a common ritual; they would even find that ritual enthusiasm builds more solidly than economic ambitions, because ritual involves a rule of life, whereas economics are a rule of gain, and so divide rather than unite.[xxvi]

This is surely a wonderful text, but it is not radical enough. Here, I think that the story of Cain is fundamental. It reveals that Cain is the founder of the first culture, but there are no specific acts of foundation in the text. What is there? The murder of Abel. Then, immediately after that, one finds the law against murder: 'if anyone kills Cain, he will suffer vengeance seven times over' (Genesis 4.15). That law represents the foundation of culture, because capital punishment is already ritual murder, and the proof of it is the stoning in Leviticus, which is a strictly regulated form of capital punishment in which the whole primitive community participates. As soon as the capital punishment is established, the repetition of the original murder is so re-enacted, i.e. a murder in which everybody takes part and for which no one is responsible. From this proto-ritual killing, then, every aspect of culture emerges: the Bible gives Cain's legacy as legal institution, domestication of animals, music, and technology (Genesis 4, 20-22).

This is exactly the equivalent of the Prometheus myth as exposed in Aeschylus.

Yes. Prometheus is the sacrificial victim who is chained and cannibalized over and over again (the eagle perpetually eats his liver) in a repetition of the sacrificial ritual. As a sacrificial victim, he is 'responsible' for the invention of culture, he is represented as the matrix from which language, mathematical science and technology emerge. The myth of Marsyas is another myth in which art and sacrifice are connected: an artistic context is ended with the slaughtering (flaying alive) of the hero. The same could be said of the only episode in the Gospel in which there is a direct reference to art: the dance of Salome in Mark: it is the dancer who decides that John the Baptist has to be beheaded.

In The Ruin of Kasch, *Calasso synthesizes the convergence of sacrificial and performative-artistic spaces in an aphoristic but effective way: 'The din of the applause drowns out the victim's cries. When the movie star or the politician is killed for being "too famous", it is said that the murderer is mad. But his madness reveals the origin of the applause.'*[xxvii]

4. CULTURAL MIMESIS AND THE ROLE OF THE OBJECT

After this general explanation of the mimetic mechanism, we would like to focus on the question of the object in your theory. For instance, you said that whenever an appetite becomes a desire it is affected by a model. Desire is completely socially constructed. However, it seems that in your general theory there is no scope for basic needs.

Let me draw a fundamental distinction: an appetite doesn't imply imitation. When someone is being choked, there is a great appetite for breathing and there isn't imitation in it because breathing is physiological. One doesn't imitate anyone when one walks for miles in a desert in order to find some water. Nonetheless, in our modern world, it is different because there are social and cultural models of fashionable eating and drinking, and any form of appetite is mediated by behavioural models, and, paradoxically, the more we do it, the more we think we are exercising 'personal', 'individual' preferences which are only our own…

The more cruel and wild a society is, the more violence is rooted in pure need. One must never exclude the possibility of violence that has nothing to do with mimetic desire but simply with scarcity. However, even at the level of basic needs, when rivalry begins and is related to an object, any kind of object, there's no doubt that it will soon become impregnated with mimesis. In these cases, there is always some social mediation at play. Marxists are convinced that certain sentiments are specifically social, since they appear in one specific social class. For them, mimetic desire is a form of aristocratic distinction, a kind of luxury. I would simply answer: of course it is! Before modern times, only the aristocrats could afford it. The theory of chivalry, for instance, is a way of glorifying mimetic desire, and Cervantes understood this perfectly. Don Quixote is an *hidalgo*, meaning 'son of someone', a man of leisure, an aristocrat. There's also no doubt that in a world of dire need, the average man has only needs and appetites. If you look at the medieval genre of the *fabliau*, it deals chiefly with physical appetites, and the struggles or fighting which occur are connected with the piece of bread which the disputants don't have. So the Marxists are partly right: if the mimetic theory denied the

objectivity of certain struggles it would be false; it would be no more than a denial of existence and its basic needs. It is no less true that mimetism, especially among those who have a knack of it, can flourish in the most extreme misery. Witness, for instance, the snobbery of Marmeladov's wife in Dostoevsky's *Crime and Punishment*.

That is why you did not accept Lucien Scubla's reading of your work, according to which 'mimetic rivalry is the only source of human violence'. [xxviii]

I agree about the essential part, although this formula undervalues objective needs and appetites too much. As I just said, basic appetites can trigger conflicts, but it is also true that the conflicts once triggered easily become trapped in a mimetic mechanism. One might say that any violent process that has any duration, any temporality, is bound to become mimetic. Nowadays there is a growing concern about 'the act of violence', meaning the random act of violence, like being robbed or mugged or raped, that could happen to anybody in the 'harmonic life' of a big city That is what people are most worried about in contemporary affluent societies. It is a violence that is totally divorced from any relational context. Therefore, it has neither antecedents nor followers. Nonetheless, specialists on violence show that haphazard aggression isn't the main cause of violence. Violent behaviour mostly occurs among people who know each other, who have known each other for a long time. [xxix] Violence has a mostly mimetic history, as in those sad cases of domestic violence. That is the most common type of crime, much more than violence between strangers. Being mugged in the street isn't directly mimetic in the sense of a relationship between the victim and the mugger, although behind random aggression there are mimetic relationships in the mugger's personal history, or in his relationship with society at large, which remain invisible but could nonetheless be discovered and explored.

We should also emphasize, however, that mimesis does not only engender disruptive effects through acquisitive mimesis, but it also allows for cultural transmission.

That is true. In the past I have mainly emphasized the rivalrous and conflictual mimesis.[xxx] I did so because I discovered the mimetic mechanism through the analysis of novels, where the representation of conflictual relations is essential. Thus, in my work, the 'bad' mimesis is always dominant, but the 'good' one is of course even more important. There would be no human mind, no education, no transmission of culture without mimesis. However, I do believe that the 'bad' mimesis needs to be emphasized because its reality remains overlooked, and it has been always neglected or mistaken for non-mimetic behaviour, and even denied by most observers. The intense capacity of humans to imitate is what forces them to become what they are, but this capacity carries a high price, with the explosion of conflicts related to acquisitive mimesis. Imitation channels not only knowledge but also violence.

A strong emphasis on positive mimesis is given in theories such as the one proposed by Richard Dawkins. His theory of memes, as a minimal unity of cultural transmission, would be a case in point.[xxxi]

Dawkins has no awareness of mimetic rivalry, mimetic crisis, scapegoating and other figures uncovered by mimetic theory. However, I think that, in general, and from my perspective, biological or neurocognitive theories of mimesis are more advanced than literary ones.

Scientists aren't afraid of developing theories and concepts which are the most relevant to the human mind and social behaviour, like imitation and mimetism, for instance, but which remain totally alien to most literary scholars and students of social sciences. Traditionally, literary studies have been grounded in the idea of individuality, on the notion of the uniqueness of a given author. Therefore, literary criticism tends to deny mimetic desire. The denial of mimetic desire and the prevalence of individualism are one and the same thing. Because the more mimetic desire one has, the more one has to be individualistic in order to deny it.

Are you suggesting that the institutionalization of literary studies helps to conceal the mechanism of mimetic desire?

Yes, absolutely. This is exactly what Sandor Goodhart affirms in *Sacrificing Commentary*.[xxxii] According to him, the real function of criticism is to bring literature back to conventional individualism, refusing and masking mimetic desire. Literary criticism has a social function which is always bringing literature back to the social norm, rather than emphasizing the gulf between the vision of a great writer and the vision of that norm. Literary criticism should help to uncover the mimetic nature of desire instead of concealing it through its engagement with concepts such as originality and novelty, constantly advocated in an incantatory and empty fashion.

Returning to the definition of mimesis: wouldn't your approach be clearer if you distinguished 'cultural mimesis' from 'acquisitive mimesis'?[xxxiii]

I don't think so. This expression would entail that cultural imitation does not involve any form of rivalry, which is not true because we could compete over cultural objects as well. Maybe we could say that mimesis has a double-bind structure, since it isn't necessarily acquisitive, in the sense of being conflictual, but also cultural. However, I fear that there is the tendency to reduce mimesis to mimicry, while only the most superficial and harmless aspects of it are stressed. That is why I have emphasized the violent side of mimesis.

We could also say that conflictual mimesis has some 'positive' aspects, because in generative terms, it engendered the social complexity of rules, taboos and social structures in order to keep violence at bay. In your anthropological account, the object usually plays the role of triggering the acquisitive mimesis. Nonetheless, is it not possible that the object can also play a fundamental role in the 'culturally peaceful mimesis'? In a historical perspective, the so-called 'hunting hypothesis of hominization' states that social groups, both animal and human, can emerge as a result of 'cooperation for hunting and the distribution of meat'.[xxxiv]

This is true. However, one has to remember that this 'good' object is killed. Hunting always has, I believe, a sacrificial dimension as well as a social dimension that cannot be generated solely by the need for hunting meat. Neither can religion be solely generated by the fear and admiration that wild animals inspire. Besides, the hunting hypothesis doesn't do justice to the role of human sacrifice.[xxxv] I think that any form of complex cooperation must be founded on some sort of cultural order, which is itself founded on the victimary mechanism. That is my hypothesis on the origins of culture. The little that is known about the prehistoric world of hunting suggests a complex cultural organization.

Of course we recognize that the originality of your approach is related to the unmasking of the acquisitive dimension of mimesis: the way in which a concrete object has a fundamental role in engendering this disruptive effect. However, as Dupuy and Dumouchel suggested, the object of the consumer society isn't exclusively the object of the acquisitive mimesis. Rather it can produce forms of controlling the explosion of mimetic rivalry.

I have no objection to this view. Dupuy and Dumouchel are fundamentally optimistic about modern society. They say that the consumer society is the way to defuse mimetic rivalry to reduce its conflictual potentiality. By making the same objects, the same commodities available to everybody, modern society has reduced the opportunity for conflict and rivalry. The problem is that if this is pushed to the extreme, as in contemporary consumer societies, then people ultimately lose all interest in these universally available and identical objects. It takes a long time for people to become disaffected, but this finally happens. The consumer society, because it renders objects available, at the same time also makes them eventually undesirable, working towards its own 'consumption'. Like all sacrificial solutions, the consumer society needs to reinvent itself periodically. It needs to dispose of more and more commodities in order to survive.[xxxvi] Moreover, the market society is devouring the earth's resources, just as primitive society devoured its victims. However, all sacrificial remedies lose their efficacy because the more available they are, the less effective they become.

Then, how should we interpret Dupuy's claim that 'the object is an actual creation of mimetic desire. That it is the composition of mimetic codetenninations which makes it appear out of nothing: it is neither the creation of an authentic freedom, nor the focal point of a blind determinism.'[xxxvii]

It goes too far in my view. First of all, I must say that if the object is entirely created by mimetic desire, it is a false object. Prestige and honour are examples of false objects created by mimetic desire. Nonetheless, there is an array of real objects for which people are competing, like two students for the same fellowship, or two physicists for the Nobel Prize.

The consumer society turns mimetic desire and its possible crisis into a positive instrument of economic wealth, but it has a side-effect: when more of the same objects are offered, they become less and less mimetically desired. This creates an inflation of objects, the consequence of which is that one now has an array of objects which go directly from the shop to the bin, with hardly a stop in between. One buys objects with one hand, and throws them away with the other – in a world where half of the human population goes hungry…

Therefore, we live in a world where the question isn't having the object but constantly shifting it.

The consumption society has simply become a system of *exchange of signs*, rather than an exchange of actual objects. That is why we live in a minimalist and anorexic world, because the world in which consumption is a sign of wealth is no longer appealing. Therefore, one has to look emaciated or subversive in order to look 'cool', as Thomas Frank would put it.[xxxviii] The only problem is that everybody resorts to the same tricks, and once again we all begin to look alike. The consumer society, at its extreme, turns us into mystics in the sense that it shows us that objects will never satisfy our desires.[xxxix] It can corrupt us in the sense that it can lead us to all sorts of useless activities, but it also brings us back to an awareness of our need for something entirely different. Something that the consumer society itself cannot provide.

At the same time, it should be remarked that the increasing level of internal mediation in contemporary society doesn't necessarily end in mimetic crisis. Our world shows itself to be quite capable of absorbing high doses of undifferentiation. Seeing this problem in primitive societies, does the scapegoat represent the return of the object? Would the corpse of the victim allow for (re)turning the doubles (in their collective form) to the previous level of differentiation?

One cannot immobilize the desire at the level of the object. That is why the non-object (not eating, exhibiting one's indifference) is so important. It isn't an invention of business, although business can always make some profit out of it. Business always prefers to sell more and more. Moreover, this formulation seems too philosophical to me, proposing a dialectic between subjectivity and objectivity that would entail a too-modern consideration of these problems, which are in fact mostly anthropological. I think we have to adhere to an anthropological appreciation of these issues. The objectiveness of the victim is precarious at that stage of the scapegoat mechanism. In the mimetic

frenzy of undifferentiation which is solved with the polarization of the victim, the corpse is eventually torn apart and consumed. This objectiveness is then immediately converted into the transcendence of the victim which is the most important aspect of the scapegoat phenomenon at this stage. What is the relationship of transcendence with the object? There is already a theological problem in that question, which is just a fascinating question in itself.

5. MÉCONNAISSANCE

To underscore the structural continuity of the social phenomena we have been discussing – in spite of the obvious historical differences they present – we could say that as much as mimetic desire isn't a modern invention, the scapegoat mechanism is not only visible in primitive rituals or ancient societies, but is also present in the modern world.

It's true, and to see how the scapegoat mechanism works in modern societies, it is necessary once more to start with mimetic desire. The paradox of mimetic desire is that it seems solidly fixed on its object, stubbornly determined to have that object and no other object, whereas in reality it very quickly shows itself to be completely opportunistic. When mimetic desire tends to become opportunistic the people affected by it focus, paradoxically, on substitute models, substitute antagonists. The age of scandals, in which we live, is a displacement of desire of this kind. A massive collective scandal corresponds to the *skandalon* of the two biblical 'neighbours' multiplied several times. Let me repeat that *skandalon* in the Gospels means *mimetic* rivalry, therefore it is that empty ambition, that ridiculous reciprocal antagonism and resentment that everybody feels for each other, for the simple reason that our desires are sometimes frustrated. When a small-scale *skandalon* becomes opportunistic, it tends to join the biggest scandal spread by the mass media, taking comfort from the fact that its indignation is shared by many people. That is, mimesis, instead of moving just in the direction of our neighbour, our specific mimetic rival, tends to become 'lateral', and this is a sign of growing crisis, of growing contagion. The biggest scandal is always devouring the smaller ones, until there is only one scandal, only one victim, and that is when the scapegoat mechanism resurfaces. The growing resentment that people feel for one another because of the increased size of the mimetic rivals conflates into a bigger resentment towards a random element of society, such as the Jews during Nazism in Germany, the Dreyfus affair in late-nineteenth-century France, the immigrants from Africa in present-day Europe, the Muslims in the recent terrorist events. A magnificent literary example of this phenomenon can be found in Shakespeare's *Julius Caesar*, in the mimetic recruiting of the conspirators against Caesar.[xl] One of them, Ligarius, is very sick, 'a feeble tongue', but at the idea of killing Caesar he revives and his floating resentment starts to focus on Caesar. He then forgets everything because now he has Caesar as the fixed point of his hatred. What progress!

Nine-tenths of politics unfortunately remembers exactly that. What people call the partisan spirit is nothing but choosing the same scapegoat as everybody else. However, because of the Christian revelation of the fundamental innocence of the scapegoat victims and the arbitrariness of the accusation against them, this polarization of hatred is soon revealed as such, and the final resolution of unanimity fails. Since I have already touched upon Christianity, let me briefly clarify my contention regarding the special place occupied by it in the history of mimetic mechanism (although most of my readers probably know about it)…

In a nutshell: before the advent of Judaism and Christianity, in one way or another, the scapegoat mechanism was accepted and justified on the basis that it remained unknown. It brought peace back to the community at the height of the chaotic mimetic crisis. All archaic religions grounded their rituals precisely around the re-enactment of the founding murder. In other words, they considered the scapegoat to be *guilty* of the eruption of the mimetic crisis. By contrast, Christianity, in the figure of Jesus, denounced the scapegoat mechanism for what it actually is: the murder of an innocent victim, killed in order to pacify a riotous community. That's the moment in which the mimetic mechanism is fully revealed.

This brings us back to the concept of méconnaissance, *which is central to the mimetic theory. You said that the 'sacrificial process requires a certain degree of misunderstanding'. If the scapegoat mechanism is to bring about social cohesion, then the innocence of the victim must be concealed in a way that allows the entire community to unite in the belief as to the victim's guilt. And you have remarked that as the actors understand the mimetic mechanism, knowing how it works, it collapses and fails to reconcile the community. However, according to Henri Atlan, this fundamental proposition is never posited as a problem. Rather, it is presented as self-evident.* [xli]

The issue here is that I did not place enough emphasis on the conscious character of the scapegoat mechanism. This is a very simple issue and, at the same time, a crucial point of my theory. Let's take, for instance, the Dreyfus affair. If you are against Dreyfus, you firmly believe Dreyfus is guilty. Imagine that you are a Frenchman in 1894, worried about the army and concerned about the Germans. If suddenly you become convinced that Dreyfus is innocent, this would destroy the spiritual comfort, the righteous anger you derive from the belief that Dreyfus is guilty. That is all I mean here! It isn't the same to be against Dreyfus as to be for him. I feel that Atlan, even though he is very astute, misunderstands what I have said. Most of the theologians who have reviewed *Things Hidden* also misunderstand this issue. There were even critics who said that if there was such a thing as a scapegoat religion, it must be Christianity, since the Gospels explicitly refer to this phenomenon! My answer is very simple: precisely because Jesus is explicitly represented as a scapegoat, Christianity as a religion cannot be founded on scapegoating; rather it is the denunciation

of it. The reason should be obvious if you believe the scapegoat is guilty, you are not going to name it as being 'my scapegoat'. If France scapegoats Dreyfus, no one will recognize that Dreyfus is a scapegoat. Everybody will only repeat that he is guilty. If you recognize the innocence of the victim, you are not going to be able to use violence so easily against that victim, and Christianity is precisely a way of saying, with maximum emphasis, that the victim is innocent. After all, the victim is the Son of God. This is the key role of the *méconnaissance* in the process – it allows one to have the illusion that one is justly accusing someone who is *really* guilty and, therefore, deserves to be punished. In order to have a scapegoat, one must fail to perceive the truth, and therefore one cannot represent the victim as a scapegoat, but rather as a righteous victim, which is what mythology does. The patricide and incest of Oedipus are supposed to be real let's not forget. To scapegoat someone is to be unaware of what you are doing.

In Shakespeare's Julius Caesar there is a remarkable speech by Brutus in which this principle is twice made explicit: 'Let us be sacrificers, but not butchers, Caius.'; 'We shall be call'd purgers, not murderers.' [xlii] *How do you interpret that?*

Brutus exalts the difference between the legitimate violence of sacrifice and the illegitimate violence of civil war, but he and his co-conspirators ultimately cannot make themselves credible as sacrificers. Brutus knows what he is doing, and he knows that to do it well he should claim that it is not a murder.

In my own vocabulary, he unmasks the necessary méconnaissance, which accompanies the killing of the scapegoat. Brutus says we must do this in such a clear fashion that it will appear as different from murder as possible. This is an incredible text with a most powerful insight. The principle is that the right hand shouldn't know what the left hand is doing. And that shows an understanding of sacrifice in Shakespeare which is extremely powerful and far superior to that of modern anthropology.

Why did you opt for the term méconnaissance *rather than the more common* 'unconscious'?

Because, in the reader's mind, the word 'unconscious' would have the Freudian connotation. I used méconnaissance because there is no doubt that one must define the scapegoat mechanism as a form of misrecognition of its injustice, without ignoring who has been killed. Now, I think that the unconscious nature of sacrificial violence is revealed in the New Testament, particularly in Luke: 'Father, forgive them, *for they do not know* what they are doing' (Luke 23.34). That sentence has to be taken literally, and the proof of it is a parallel statement in the Acts of the Apostles. Peter, addressing the crowd who had been present at the crucifixion, says 'you acted in ignorance' (Acts 3.17).[xliii] The word 'ignorance' is really the Greek word for 'not knowing'. But in our contemporary language one has to say 'unconscious'. However, I do not want to say the unconscious with the definite article because it implies a form of ontological essentialism that I distrust. However, there

is definitely a lack of consciousness in scapegoating, and this lack of consciousness is as essential as the unconscious is in Freud. However, it isn't the same thing and it is collective rather than individual.

Could you then clarify your criticism of Freud's concept of the unconscious?

What I'm against is the idea that there is *an* unconscious, as a separate mental entity. There isn't anything wrong with the idea of something being unconscious, but the idea of *the* unconscious, as a kind of 'black box', has been proved misleading. As I just said, I should have placed more emphasis on the unconscious nature of the scapegoat mechanism, but I refuse to lock it up into an unconscious that has a life of its own, in the style of Freud. In Freud, the unconscious also has a collective structure, but it is indeed basically composed of individual experiences. Regarding interdividual psychology, the *méconnaissance* seems also to prevent the recognition of the mimetic nature of desire.

Do you think that the more mimetic one is, the stronger the méconnaissance *will be?*

I will answer with a paradox. The more you are mimetic, the stronger is your méconnaissance and also the possibilities of understanding it. Suddenly you can realize that the nature of your own desire is strictly imitative. I believe all great writers of mimetic desire are hyper-mimetic. As I tried to show in my books, Proust and Dostoevsky, for instance, are extraordinary examples of this. In their novels, there is a radical break between the mediocrity of their early works, which are attempts of self-justification, and the greatness of their later works, which all represent the fall of the self, in the sense of Camus' last book, *La Chute*. I think *La Chute* is a book about the bad faith of modern writers, who condemn the entire creation in order to justify themselves and build a fortress of illusory moral superiority.

How would you define a hyper-mimetic person?

Authors such as Proust or Shakespeare obviously talk about themselves. Take the relationship of Proust's narrator with Albertine. The mechanical nature of the mimetic desire is so obvious (to the point of caricature): when she is absent, he is in love with her; when she is present, he is no longer interested. It doesn't just happen once or twice, it happens so many times that it begins to look like a scientific experiment. It is reminiscent also of the relationship between Kafka and Felice, as revealed in their correspondence. One of the best essays on Kafka is by Elias Canetti.[xliv] It is a text about the mimetic Kafka which is intensely comical. In Freudian terms, it would have been described as an analysis of Kafka's neurosis. However, it is an essay on Kafka as an absolutely hyper-mimetic man, and Canetti seems to have understood that in a powerful way.

We could say that if one is hyper-mimetic, one is in a better position to understand oneself as a puppet of mimetic desire, simply because the caricature one has become makes it easier to understand the systematically self-defeating nature of one's own behaviour. In its mechanical nature it is quite close to the demonic possession cited in the Gospels.

Then is a hyper-mimetic person someone who has a special sensitivity to the mimetic mechanism?

Yes. In my view, there are two types of hyper-mimetic men: those who are totally blind to their own mimetism, and those who become totally lucid. What is so interesting about Dostoevsky – and to a large extent the Proust of *Jean Santeuil* – is that, in his first works, Dostoevsky is totally blind about himself. He is a caricature of his mimetic desire, and he idealizes his mimetic reactions. If one reads Dostoevsky's correspondence, one can see that it could be totally interchangeable with his novels of the early period. Then, suddenly, with *Notes from Underground*, he had his great insight.[xlv] But he doesn't unveil the mimetic mechanism in the way that Shakespeare did. He is the equal of Shakespeare in many things, but Shakespeare is more knowledgeable with respect to the mimetic mechanism and its power to regenerate archaic societies. Shakespeare is surely closer to our present anthropological research than Dostoevsky. *A Midsummer Night's Dream* is incredibly powerful on this score, so much so that even great writers such as George Orwell cannot grasp it, accusing Shakespeare of superficiality! Orwell does not realize how this work rises above its characters and their minuscule childish actions. He fails to grasp its generative dimension.

i. This text was published in *Evolution and Conversion: Dialogues on the Origins of Culture*, René Girard with Pierpaolo Antonello and João Cezar de Castro Rocha, T & T Clark, London, 2007. (ed.)

ii. See Girard, *Things Hidden*, Book III, Chapter 2: 'Desire without Object', pp. 299-305.

iii. See, for instance, Andrew N. Meltzoff and M. Keith Moore, 'Want Intersubjectivity: Broadening the dialogue to include imitation, identity and intention', in Stein Braten (ed.), *Intersubjective Communication and Emotion in Early Ontogeny*, Cambridge: Cambridge University Press, 1998, pp. 47-62; A.N. Meltzoff and M.K. Moore, 'Persons and Representation: Why infant imitation is important for theories of human development', in J. Nadel and G. Butterworth (eds.), *Imitation in Infancy*, Cambridge: Cambridge University Press, 1999, pp. 9-35; A.N. Meltzoff and A. Gopnik, 'The Role of Imitation in Understanding Persons and Developing a Theory of Mind', in S. Baron-Cohen, H. Tager-Flusberg and D.J. Cohen (eds.), *Understanding Other Minds*, Oxford: Oxford University Press, 1993, pp. 335-66.

iv. At the COV&R meeting in Saint Denis, Paris: 'Education, Mimesis, Violence and Reduction of Violence', 27-30 May1998. Ricoeur also presented a paper on 'Religion and Symbolic Violence', later published in *Contagion*, 6 (1999): 1-11.

v. The image of the mirror is in Alcibiades, 133a; *Timaeus*, 46a; Plato, Epigrams, 11; Sophist, 239d. In the *Republic*, Plato describes unbounded imitation as an actual crisis of doubles: Republic, III, 395e-396b. Girard already referred to this idea in *Things Hidden*, p. 15. See also Giuseppe Fornari, *Fra Dioniso e Cristo. La sapienza sacrificale greca e la civiltà occidentale* (Bologna: Pitagora, 2001), 389-91. Derrida, in the chapter 'The Double Session', in *Dissemination*, remarks that in the Republic, Plato says that Homer 'is condemned because he practises mimesis (or mimetic, rather than simple diegesis)' while on the contrary Parmenides 'is condemned because he neglects mimesis. If violence must be done on him, it is because his logos, the "paternal thesis", would prohibit (one from accounting for) the proliferation of the doubles ("idols, icons, likeness, semblances")… (*Sophist*, 241d-e).' Jacques Derrida, *La Dissemination*, Paris: Editions du Seuil, 1972, trans. with Intro. and notes by Barbara Johnson, *Dissemination*, Chicago, IL: University of Chicago Press, 1981, p. 186.

vi. Girard, *Violence and the Sacred*, p. 169ff.

vii. A conference, 'Perspective on Imitation. From cognitive neuroscience to social sciences', was held at the Royaumont Abbey, 24-26 May 2002.

viii. See, for instance, A. Meltzoff, 'Foundations for Developing a Concept of Self: the role of imitation in relating self to other and the value of social mirroring, social modeling, and self practice in infancy', in D. Chicchetti and M. Beeghly (eds), *The Self in Transition: Infancy to Childhood*, Chicago, IL: Chicago University Press, 1990, pp. 139-64.

ix. See, for instance, G. Rizzolati, L. Fogassi and V. Gallese, 'Neurophysiological mechanisms underlying the understanding and imitation of action', *Nature Reviews Neuroscience*, 2, (2001): 661-70.

x. See R. Girard and Michel Serres, *Le Tragique et la pitié. Discours de réception de René Girard a 1'Académie Française et réponse de Michel Serres*, Paris: Le Pommier, 2006.

xi. 'I have personally watched and studied a jealous baby. He could not speak and, pale with jealousy and bitterness, glared at his brother sharing his mother's milk. Who is unaware of this fact of experience?' (I, 11). Saint Augustine, *Confessions*, trans. Henry Chadwick, Oxford University Press, p. 9.

xii. There is a quite candid but sharp comment in one of Andy Warhol's books: What's great about this country is that America started the tradition where the richest consumers buy essentially the same thing as the poorest. You can be watching TV and see Coca-Cola, and you can know that the President drinks Coke, Liz Taylor drinks Coke, and just think, you can drink Coke, too. A Coke is a Coke and no amount of money can get you a better Coke than the one the bum on the corner is drinking. (A. Warhol, *The Philosophy of Andy Warhol [From A to B and Back Again]*, San Diego, CA: Harcourt Brace, 1975, pp. 100-1.)

xiii. See Girard, *Le Sacrifice*.

xiv. See Girard, *I See Satan Fall Like Lightning*, pp. 7-8.

xv. The version of the Bible here quoted is the New International Version. We will refer to this version throughout the book.

xvi. On this issue, see Paul Dumouchel and Jean-Pierre Dupuy (eds.), *L'auto-organisation. De la Physique au politique,* Paris: Editions du Seuil, 1983, p. 283ff.

xvii. See Plato's *Republic*, II, 361b-362a: 'a just person in such circumstances will be whipped, stretched on a rack, chained, blinded with fire, and, at the end, when he has suffered every kind of evil, he'll be impaled, and will realize then that one shouldn't want to be just but to be believed to be just.' See also Fornari, *Fra Dioniso e Cristo*, p. 375.

xviii. Evidence of Plato's trip of can be found in Diogenes Laertius. See Diogenes Laertius, *Lives, Teachings and Sayings of Famous Philosophers,* III, 6. I owe this remark to Giuseppe Fornari.

xix. F. Nietzsche, *Twilight of the Idols*, trans. R.J. Hollingdale, London: Penguin, 1968, p. 117: 'I find [Plato] deviated so far from all the fundamental instincts of the Hellenes, so morally infected, so much an antecedent Christian… It has cost us dear that this Athenian went to school with the Egyptians (-or with the Jews in Egypt?…).

xx. Carlo Ginzburg shows this widespread connection between limping, or limb mutilations of some sort, in mythological figures with ritual killing and the world of death. However, he does not take the scapegoat hypothesis into serious consideration. Cf. C. Ginzburg, *Storia notturna. Una decifrazione del sabba*, Einaudi, 1989, pp. 206-75.

xxi. See Girard, *Things Hidden*, Book I, Chapter 2; 'The Development of Culture and Institutions', in particular, pp. 51-8, 'Sacred Kingship and Central Power'.

xxii. Arthur Maurice Hocart, *Kings and Councilors* (1936) (Chicago, IL: University of Chicago Press, 1970), p. 12ff. Hocart in particular refers to the popular prejudice of historians and students of culture who pin their 'faith to direct evidence, to the writings of eyewitnesses, to coins, to ruins'. For further discussion on this subject, see Ch. 5.

xxiii. Girard, *Things Hidden*, pp. 100-1.

xxiv. Roger Caillois groups games according to four features: agon, alea, mimicry, ilinx.

xxv. For a full analysis of the image of labyrinth in Greek mythology from a mimetic standpoint, see G. Fornari, 'Labyrinthine strategies of sacrifice: The Cretans by Euripides', *Contagion*, 4 (1997): 163-88.

xxvi. Hocart, *Kings and Councilors*, p. 35.

xxvii. Roberto Calasso, *La Rovina di kasch* (Milan: Adelphi, 1983), p. 192.

xxviii. Lucien Scubla, 'Contribution à la théorie du sacrifice', in M. Deguy and J.-P. Dupuy (eds.), *René Girard et le problème du mal*, (Paris: Grasset, 1982), p. 105.

xxix. A recent report from the World Health Organization on violent death in 80 different countries, explains that half of them are caused by suicide, while the majority of homicides are committed within the family. Only one-fifth of violent deaths every year are caused by war. See *World Report on Violence and Health* (Geneva: World Health Organization, 2002).

xxx. See Girard, *Things Hidden*, pp. 15-19.

xxxi. Richard Dawkins, *The Selfish Gene* (Oxford and New York: Oxford University Press, 1976).

xxxii. Sandor Goodhart, *Sacrificing Commentary: Reading the End of Literature* (Baltimore, MD: Johns Hopkins University Press, 1996).

xxxiii. In a different context, Leonardo Boff addresses a similar issue: I still think that the other pole of mimetic desire should be more emphasized. I'm referring to the desire that brings goodness into history. On the one hand, there is a mimetic mechanism that produces victims and creates a historical culture grounded on victims. On the other hand, and at the same time, there is an inclusive desire, which looks for a 'solidary' mimetism, committed to making historically possible the production of goodness and life. (In H. Assmann (ed.) *René Girard com teólogos da libertaçao, Um dialogo sobre idolos e sacrificios* [Petrópolis: Editora Vozes, 1991] pp. 56-7).

xxxiv. Walter Burkert, 'The Problem of Ritual Killing', in Robert Hamerton-Kelly (ed.), *Violent Origins. Ritual Killing and Cultural Formation* (Stanford: Stanford University Press, 1987), p. 164.

xxxv. See Girard and Burkert's discussion, *ibid.*, pp. 177-88.

xxxvi. Daniel Miller, in his book *A Theory of Shopping* (Cambridge: Polity Press, 1998), speaks of shopping as sacrifice, although it is mostly confined to Bataille's perspective: 'The discourse of shopping is purely destructive, a marvelous envisaging of complete waste. It captures the transgressive potentiality of money itself, explored by Simmel and others, as social liberation from considerations of particularity' (p. 95).

xxxvii. J.-P. Dupuy, 'Mimesis et morphogenèse', in Deguy and Dupuy (eds.), *René Girard et le problème du mal*, p. 232.

xxxviii. Thomas Frank, *The Conquest of Cool: Business Culture, Counterculture, and the Rise of Hip Consumerism* (Chicago, IL: University of Chicago Press, 1997). Frank claims that an important marketing phenomenon, which started in the 1960s, is the so-called 'commodification of discontent', meaning selling people signs of their disaffection from the very system that sells them.

xxxix. Dupuy also refers to capitalism as the most 'spiritual' of universes, because its concern is not strictly materialistic (as Max Weber's sociological analysis claimed) meaning the sheer acquisition of objects, but it is based on envy. Objects are 'signs of envy' in which the role of the mediator, of the other, is always present. See J.-P. Dupuy, 'Le Signe et l'envie', in Dumouchel and Dupuy, *L'Auto-organisation*, p. 74

xl. See *Julius Caesar*, II, i. See also Girard, *A Theatre of Envy*, pp. 308-9.

xli. Henri Atlan, 'Violence fondatrice et référent divin', in P. Dumouchel (ed.), *Violence et vérité. Autour de René Girard* (Paris: Grasset, 1985), pp. 434-50.

xlii. William Shakespeare, *Julius Caesar*, ACT II, l. 166, 180. For an analysis of that passage, see René Girard, 'Let us be Sacrificers, but not Butchers, Caius. Sacrifice in *Julius Caesar*', in Girard, *A Theatre of Envy*, pp. 210-19.

xliii. Cf. Girard, *I See Satan*, pp. 126-7. Some early manuscripts do not have Luke's sentence.

xliv. Elias Canetti, *Der andere Prozess* (Munich: Carl Hanser, 1969), trans. Christopher Middleton, *Kafka's Other Trial. The Letters to Felice* (New York: Schocken, 1974). See, for instance, pp. 16-17: I'm jealous of all the people in your letter, those named and those unnamed, men and girls, business people and writers (writers above all, needless to say)... I'm jealous of Werfel, Sophocles, Ricarda Huch, Lagerlof, Jacobsen. My jealousy is childishly pleased because you call Eulenberg Hermann instead of Herbert, while Franz no doubt is deeply engraved on your brain... But other people are to be found in your letter as well; I want to start a fight with them all, the whole lot, not because I mean to do them any harm, but to drive them away from you, to get you away from them, to read only letters that are concerned solely with you, your family and of course, of course, me! The following day he receives a letter from her that is unexpected, for it is Sunday, and he thanks her: 'Dearest, once again this is the kind of letter that makes one go hot with silent joy. It isn't full of all those friends and writers'.

xlv. For a detailed discussion on this issue, see René Girard, *Dostoyevsky: du double à l'unité* (Paris: Plon, 1963), trans. James G. Williams, *Resurrection from the Underground* (New York: Crossroad, 1997).

Innovation & Repetition

René Girard

"Innovation", from the Latin *innovare*, *innovatio*, should signify renewal, rejuvenation from inside, rather than novelty, which is its modern meaning in both English and French. Judging from the examples in the Oxford English Dictionary and the Littré, the word came into widespread use only in the sixteenth century and, until the eighteenth century, its connotations were almost uniformly unfavourable.

In the vulgar tongues, as well as in medieval Latin, the word is used primarily in theology, and it means a departure from what by definition should not change – religious dogma. In many instances, innovation is practically synonymous with heresy. Orthodoxy is unbroken continuity and, therefore, the absence of innovation.

This is how Bossuet defines the orthodoxy of the great ecumenical councils: "On n'innovait rien à Constantinople," he writes, "mais on n'avait pas plus innové à Nicée" (Nothing was innovated at Constantinople, but nothing was innovated at Nicea either).

All uses of the word are patterned on the rheological. Good things are stable by definition and therefore untainted with innovation, which is always presented as dangerous or suspicious. In politics, innovation is almost tantamount to rebellion and revolution. As we might expect, Hobbes loathes innovation. In *Government and Society* (1651), he writes:

> *There are many who supposing themselves wiser than others,*
> *endeavour to innovate, and diverse innovators innovate in various ways.*

Besides theology and politics, language and literature seem threatened by unwanted innovation, especially in "classical" France. The seventeenth-century French grammarians and literary theoreticians are against innovation, of course. Here are two mediocre lines of Ménage:

> N'innovez ni ne faites rien
> En la langue et vous ferez bien.

> *(Don't innovate or do anything*
> *to the language, and you will do well.)*

Hostility to innovation is what we expect from conservative thinkers, but we are surprised to find it under the pen of authors whom we regard as innovators. When Calvin denounces "l'appétit et convoitise de tout innover, changer et remuer" (the appetite and desire to innovate, change, and stir up everything), he sounds just like Bossuet. So does Cromwell in 1658, when he attacks what he calls "Designs … laid to innovate upon the Civil Rights of Nations, and to innovate in matters of religion."

The reformers see the Reformation not as innovation but as a restoration of original Christianity. They profess to return to the authentic imitation of Christ, uncorrupted by Catholic innovation.

Mutatis mutandis – the humanists feel just like the Protestants. They, too, hate innovation. More than ever, they look back to the ancient models that the Middle Ages revered. They indict their medieval predecessors not on the grounds that they selected the wrong models but that they did not imitate the right ones properly. The humanists differ from the Protestants, of course, in that, instead of being religious, their models are the philosophers, writers, and artists of classical antiquity.

Montaigne hates innovation. "Rien ne presse un estat," he writes, "que l'innovation; le changement donne seul forme à l'injustice et à la tyrannie." (Nothing harries a state except innovation; change alone gives form to injustice and tyranny). In the *Essays*, innovation is synonymous with "nouvelleté", a word which the author also uses disparagingly.

A social and political component is present in all this fear of the new, but something else lies behind it, something religious that is more archaic and pagan than specifically Christian. The negative view of innovation reflects what I call external mediation, a world in which the need for and the identity of all cultural models is taken for granted. This is so true that, in the Middle Ages, the concept of innovation is hardly needed. Its use is usually confined to technical discussions of heresy in Latin. In the vulgar tongues, the need for the word appears only in the last phase of external mediation, which I roughly identify with the sixteenth and seventeenth centuries.

People mutually accuse each other of being bad imitators, unfaithful to the true essence of the models. Not until a little later, with the great *querelle des anciens et des modernes*, does the battle shift to the question of which models are best, the traditional ones or their modern rivals?

The idea that there must be models still remains common to both camps. The principle of stable imitation is the foundation of the system, and is the last to be questioned.

The world of external mediation genuinely fears the loss of its transcendental models. Society is felt to be inherently fragile. Any tampering with things as they are could unleash the primordial mob and bring about a regression to original chaos. What is feared is a collapse of religion and society as a whole, through a mimetic contagion that would turn the people into a mob.

We have many echoes of this in Shakespeare. In Henry IV, Part I, the King speaks of "poor discontents, Which gape and rub the elbow at the news Of hurlyburly innovation" (V.1.76-78).

"Hurlyburly" means tumult, confusion, storm, violent upheaval. In 1639, Webster mentions: "The Hydra-headed multitude that only gape for innovation." On the subject of the English revolution, Bossuet speaks a similar language and reflects a similar mentality:

> Quelque chose de plus violent se
> remuait dans le fond des coeurs;
> c'était un dégoût secret de tout ce qui
> a de l'autorité, et une démangeaison
> d'innover sans fin dès qu'on en a vu
> le premier exemple.

> *(Something very violent stirred in the bottom*
> *of their hearts; it was a secret disgust of everything*
> *having authority, and an urge to innovate*
> *incessantly from the moment of*
> *seeing a first example of it.)*

A taste for innovation is supposed to denote a perverse and even a deranged mind. The unfavourable implications of the word were so well established that we still find them under the pen of a thinker as radical as Diderot: "Toute innovation est à craindre dans un gouvernement" (In a government, every innovation is to be feared). There is an apocalyptic ring to this old use of innovation that contrasts sharply with the modern flavour of the term.

The Jacobin Terror was such, it seems, as to keep this fear alive, but only the most eloquent traditionalists can play the old tune successfully – Xavier de Maistre, and, on occasion, Edmund Burke. He calls the French Revolution "a revolt of innovation; and thereby the very elements of society have been confounded and dissipated."

Paradoxically, the Revolution did not reinforce the ancient fear of *innovation*, but instead greatly contributed to its demise. The guillotine terrified many people, of course, but it was "political" terror in the modern sense and no longer something mysterious and uncanny. What disappeared at that time is the feeling that any deliberate tinkering with the social order is not only sacrilegious but intrinsically perilous, likely to trigger an apocalyptic disaster.

Even if the bad connotations of our word occasionally resurfaced in the eighteenth century, the story of the hour was not the perpetuation of the past, but its overthrow. It is not the core *meaning* of "innovation" that changed, but its affective "aura".

The reason, of course, was the shift away from theology, and even philosophy, toward science and technology. The word was interpreted in a new context which caused examples of brilliant and useful inventions to spring to the mind. The good impression automatically spilled over into areas and disciplines unrelated to science and technology. This process exactly reversed the earlier one, when the bad connotations rooted in theology extended to the non-theological uses of the word.

In his *Histoire philosophe* (1770), Abbé Raynal rehabilitated innovation through the contextual change just defined. In typical philosophe style, he discarded the theological background with alacrity. Addressing his reader directly, the abbé writes:

Tu entendras murmurer autour de toi:
cela ne se peut,
et quand cela se pourrait,
ce sont des innovations; des innovations!
Soit, mais tant de découvertes dans les sciences
et dans les arts n'en ont-elles pas été.

(You will hear murmured all around,
that's not possible,
and when that would be possible,

it's innovations, innovations!
Right, but so many discoveries in the sciences
and in the arts, haven't they been innovations?)

All it takes to nip intelligent reforms in the bud is to brandish this old scarecrow, "innovation." The very sound of the word has been so unpleasant, traditionally, that no further argument is needed. Since inventions in the arts and the sciences are also innovations, the bad connotations are unfounded, and should be replaced by good ones. At the time Raynal was writing, the change he advocated was occurring. The foul smell of heresy finally dissipated and was instantly replaced by the inebriating vapours of scientific and technical progress.

From then on, in all walks of life, would-be innovators leaned upon the prestige of science in order to promote their views. This is especially true in the political and social sphere. Social organization is now perceived as the creation of mere human beings, and other human beings have the right to redesign it in part or even *in toto*.

As early as the beginning of the nineteenth century, innovation became the god that we are still worshipping today. In 1817, for instance, Bentham characterized an idea as "a proposition so daring, so innovational...!" (Someone must have found innovative too short a word, and forged the longer "innovational." That someone must have been Bentham himself. Innovation to him is like candy to a child – the bigger the piece, the more slowly and voluptuously it will dissolve in the mouth.)

The new cult meant that a new scourge had descended upon the World – "stagnation". Before the eighteenth century, "stagnation" was unknown; suddenly, it spread its gloom far and wide. The more innovative the capitals of the modern spirit became, the more "stagnant" and "boring" the surrounding countryside appeared. In *La Rabouilleuse* (1842), a supposedly conservative Balzac deplores the retrograde ways of the French provinces: "Hélas! Faire comme faisaient nos pères, ne rien innover, telle est la loi du pays" (Alas! To do things as our fathers did, to innovate nothing, such is the law of the countryside).

In an amazingly short time, a systematically positive view of innovation replaced the systematically negative one. Everything was reversed, and even the least innovative people found themselves celebrating innovation.

INNOVATION AND IMITATION

As in most semantic revolutions, rhetoric plays a role, but more than rhetoric is involved. The world that reviled innovation was changing very fast, faster, no doubt, than at any previous time in its history, but the world that exalts innovation has been changing even faster.

Our little revolution coincides with two big ones that have not yet completed their course: the democratic revolution and the industrial revolution. The latter is rooted in a third, the scientific revolution, which started earlier, no doubt, but whose pace greatly accelerated when the other two also picked up steam.

As I said before, the negative view of innovation is inseparable from a conception of the spiritual and intellectual life dominated by stable imitation. Being the source of eternal truth, of eternal beauty, of eternal goodness, the models should never change. Only when these transcendental models are toppled can innovation acquire a positive meaning. *External mediation* gives way to a world in which, at least in principle, individuals and communities are free to adopt whichever models they prefer and, better still, no model at all.

This seems to go without saying. Our world has always believed that "to be innovative" and "to be imitative" are two incompatible attitudes. This was already true when innovation was feared; now that it is desired, it is truer than ever.

The following sentence is a good example. Michelet deplores the influence of moderate elements on the French Revolution: "Ils la firent réformatrice, l'empêchèrent d'être fondatrice, d'innover et de créer" (They made it reformatory, prevented it from being a new foundation, from innovating and creating). The romantic historian puts innovation on a par with foundation and creation itself, the creation *ex nihilo*, no doubt, that, up to that time, had been the exclusive monopoly of the biblical God.

During the nineteenth and much of the twentieth centuries, as the passion for innovation intensified, the definition of it becomes more and more radical, less and less tolerant of tradition, that is, of imitation. As it spread from painting to music and to literature, the radical view of innovation triggered the successive upheavals that we call "modern art." A complete break with the past is viewed as the sole achievement worthy of a "creator".

At least in principle, this innovation mania affects all aspects of human existence. This is true not only of such movements as surrealism, but of writers who, at first sight, seem to continue more traditional trends.

Consider, for instance, the implications of the following sentence in Raymond Radiguet's *Le Diable au corps*: "Tous les amants, même les plus médiocres, s'imaginent qu'ils innovent" (All lovers, even the most mediocre, believe that they innovate). If the novelist finds it necessary to say that the innovation of mediocre lovers is imaginary, he must also believe that it can be real, when it proceeds from genuinely talented lovers.

Just as the measure of a painter's talent is now his capacity to innovate in painting, the measure of a lover's love is his or her capacity to innovate in the field of love-making. To be "with it" in the France of 1920, one had to be "innovative" even in the privacy of the boudoir. What a burden on all lovers' shoulders! Far from exorcising the urge to mimic famous lovers in literature and history, compulsory innovation can only inflame it further.

Even philosophy succumbed to the "terrorism" of innovation. When French philosophers began to look for an insurance policy against the greatest possible ill-fidelity to the past, the repetition of *dépassé* philosophies – one of their inventions was *la rupture épistémologique*. This miraculous concept made it possible for the communist Althusser to be an old-style apparatchik on the one hand and, on the other, one hundred percent innovational, almost as much so as Marx himself, since Althusser was the first to take the full measure of the prophet's innovative genius.

The psychoanalyst Lacan pulled exactly the same trick with Freud. Very quickly, however, one single *rupture épistémologique* for all times and for all people seemed paltry. Each thinker had to have his own, and then the really chic thinkers had several in a row. In the end, everybody turned themselves into a continuous and monstrous rupture, not primarily with others – that goes without saying – but with one's own past.

This is how *inconsistency* has become the major intellectual virtue of the avant-garde. But the real credit for the *tabula rasa* school of innovation should go to Nietzsche, who was tired of repeating with everybody else that a great thinker should have no model. He went one better, as always, and made the refusal to *be* a model the mark of genius. This is still a sensation that is being piously repeated every day. Nietzsche is our supreme model of model repudiation, our revered guru of guru-renunciation.

The emphasis on *ruptures*, *fragments*, and *discontinuities* is still all the rage in our universities. Michel Foucault has taught us to cut up the history of ideas in separate segments with no communication between them. Even the history of science has developed its own counterpart of Foucault's *épistémé*. In the *Structure of Scientific Revolution*, Thomas Kuhn tells us more or less that the only scientists worth their salt are those who make themselves completely unintelligible to their colleagues by inventing an entirely new *paradigm*.

This extreme view of *innovation* has been dominant for so long that even our dictionaries take it for granted. *Innovation* is supposed to exclude *imitation* as completely as imitation excludes it. Examples of how the word should be used are of this type: "It is easier to imitate than to innovate."

This conception is false, I believe, but its falsity is easier to show in some domains than in others. The easiest illustration is to be seen in contemporary market economies. This is certainly a domain in which innovation occurs on a massive, even a frightening scale, at least in the so-called developed countries. It is not difficult to observe the type of behaviour that fosters economic innovation. In economics, innovation has a precise definition; it is sometimes the bringing of a technical invention into widespread practical use, but it can be many other things, such as improvements in production technique, or in management. It is anything yet untried that gives a business an edge over its competitors. That is why innovation is often regarded as the principal, even the sole source, of profits.

Business people can speak lyrically about their mystical faith in innovation and the brave new world it is creating, but the driving force behind their constant innovation is far from utopian. In a vigorous economy, it is a matter of survival, pure and simple. Business firms must innovate in order to remain competitive.

Competition, from two Latin words, *cum* and *petere*, means to "seek together". What all businessmen seek is profits; they seek them together with their competitors in the paradoxical relationship that we call "competitive".

When a business loses money it must innovate very fast, and it cannot do so without forethought. Usually there is neither the money nor the time for this. In this predicament, business people with a strong survival instinct will usually reason as follows: "If our competitors are more successful than we are, they must be doing something right. We must do it ourselves, and the only practical way to go about it is to imitate them as exactly as we can."

Most people will agree that there is a role for imitation in economic recovery, but only in the first phase of the healing process. By imitating its successful competitors, an endangered firm can innovate in relation to itself; it will thus catch up with its rivals, but it will invent nothing really new.

This common sense makes less sense than it seems. To begin with, is there such a thing as "absolute innovation"? In a first phase, no doubt, imitation will be rigid and myopic. It will have the ritual quality of external mediation. After a while, however, the element of novelty in the competitor's practice will be mastered, and imitation will become bolder. At that moment, it may – or may not – generate some additional improvement, which will seem insignificant at first, because it is not suggested by the model, but which really is the genuine innovation that will turn things around.

I am not denying the specificity of innovation. I am simply observing that, concretely, in a truly innovative process, it is often so continuous with imitation that its presence can be discovered only after the fact, through a process of abstraction that isolates aspects which are inseparable from one another.

Not so long ago, in Europe, the Americans were portrayed as primarily imitators, good technicians, no doubt, but the real brain power was in Germany or in England. Then, in very few years, the Americans became great innovators.

Public opinion is always surprised when it sees the modest imitators of one generation turn into the daring innovators of the next. The constant recurrence of this phenomenon must have something to teach us.

Until quite recently, the Japanese were dismissed as mere copiers of Western ways, incapable of real leadership in any field. They are now the driving force behind innovation in more and more technical fields. When did they acquire that inventive spark which, supposedly, they lacked? At this very moment, imitators of the Japanese – the Koreans, the Taiwanese – are repeating the same process. They, too, are fast turning into innovators. Had not something similar already occurred in the nineteenth century, when Germany first rivalled and then surpassed England in industrial might? The metamorphosis of imitators into innovators occurs repeatedly, but we always react to it with amazement. Perhaps we do not want to know about the role of imitation in innovation.

"It is easier to imitate than to innovate." This is what the dictionaries tell us. But it is true that the only shortcut to innovation is imitation. And here is another sentence that illustrates the meaning of innovation: "Many people imitate when they think that they innovate." This cannot be denied, but it should be added that many people innovate when they think that they imitate.

INNOVATION AND COMPETITION

In economic life, imitation and innovation are not only compatible but almost inseparable. This conclusion runs counter to the modern ideology of absolute innovation. Does it mean that this precious commodity comes in two varieties, one that relies on imitation and one that does not, a lower type reserved for business and a "higher" type reserved for "higher" culture?

This is what many intellectuals want to believe. If we agreed with them, we would nullify the one great insight of Marx – that the same competitive pattern dominates all aspects of modern culture, being the most visible in economic life. On this particular point, Marx is our best guide.

The radical view of innovation is obviously false. But why does our culture so stubbornly cling to it? Why are modern intellectuals and artists so hostile to imitation?

In order to answer this question, we must go back to our example of mimetic inventiveness – business competition. The very fact that those who compete are models and imitators shows two things: imitation survives the collapse of external mediation; and a crucial change has occurred in its *modus operandi*.

In "external mediation" either the models have the advantage of being long dead or of standing so far above their imitators that they cannot become their rivals. This is not the case in the modern world. Since competitors stand next to each other, in the same world, they must all compete for the things that they desire in common, with resulting reciprocal imitation. This is the great difference between "external" and "internal" mediation.

All imitators select models whom they regard as superior. In "internal mediation", models and imitators are equal in every respect except one: the superior achievement of the one, which motivates the imitation of the other. This means, of course, that the models are successful *at their imitators' expense*.

Defeat in any kind of competition is disagreeable for reasons that go beyond the material losses that may be incurred. When we imitate successful rivals, we explicitly acknowledge what we would prefer to deny – their superiority. The urge to imitate is very strong, since it opens up possibilities of bettering the competition. But the urge *not* to imitate is also very strong. The only thing that the losers can deny the winners is the homage of their imitation.

Unlike external mediation, the internal variety is a reluctant *mimesis* that generally goes un-recognized because it hides behind a bewildering diversity of masks. The mimetic urge can never be repressed entirely, but it can turn into counter-imitation. The losers try to demonstrate their independence by systematically taking the course opposite to that of the winners.

Thus, they may act in a way detrimental to their own self-interest. Their pride turns self-destructive. No political or Freudian "unconscious" is necessary to account for that.

Even in economic life, where the material incentives to imitate are strongest, the urge *not* to imitate may prove even stronger, especially in international trade, which is affected by questions of "national pride." When a nation cannot successfully compete, it is tempted to blame its failure on unfair competition, thus paving the way for protectionist measures that put an end to peaceful competition.

INNOVATION IN THE ARTS

The rules of the game may be objectively unfair, of course, but they never seem so to the winners and they always seem so to the losers. Nations greatly dislike the image of themselves projected by any kind of defeat, and they will try to efface it by all possible means. If they feel that it cannot be done through fair competition, they may resort to violence or retreat into the sterile isolation of *autarkie*.

It is not a deficit but an *excess* of competitive spirit that makes productive competition impossible. If this occasionally happens in economic life, where the incentive to compete is greatest, what about more subtle and hidden but even more intense forms of competition, like in the sciences, the arts, and philosophy, where universally acknowledged means of evaluation are lacking?

In my opinion, the tendency to define "innovation" in more and more "radical" and anti-mimetic terms – the mad escalation that I briefly sketched earlier – reflects a vast surrender of modern intelligence

to this mimetic pressure, a collective embrace of self-deception which Marx himself, for all his insights, remarkably exemplifies. Like many nineteenth – and twentieth – century intellectuals, Marx sees competitiveness as an unmitigated evil that can and should be abolished, together with the free market, the only economic system that, for all its faults, channels the competitive spirit into constructive efforts instead of exacerbating it to the level of physical violence or discouraging it entirely. Marx's purely historical thinking misses the complex anthropological consequences of democratic equality which Tocqueville perceived. Marx did not detect the change from one modality of imitation to another; he was unable to define the mimetic rivalry unleashed by the abandonment of transcendental models, by the collapse of hierarchical thinking. In spite of many glorious exceptions, our recent intellectual climate has been determined not by a lucid analysis of these phenomena, but by their repression, which produces the type of effects described by Nietzsche as *ressentiment*. Most intellectuals take the path of least intellectual resistance vis-à-vis internal mediation, and their obsessive concern with their own mimetic rivals is always accompanied by a fierce denial of participation in mimetic rivalry and a determination to crush this abomination through the means of political and cultural revolution.

As a result, most theories fashionable in Europe in the nineteenth and twentieth centuries have been philosophical and aesthetic equivalents of the economic *autarkie* that preceded World War II, and their consequences have been no less disastrous. The urge to imitate successful rivals is so abhorrent that all forms of mimesis must be discredited. Instead of re-examining imitation and discovering its conflictual dimension, the eternal avant-garde has waged a purely defensive and ultimately self-destructive war against it.

When the *humility* of discipleship is experienced as *humiliating*, the transmission of the past becomes difficult, even impossible. The so-called counter-culture of the sixties was a climactic moment in this strange rebellion, a revolt not merely against the competitiveness of modern life in all its forms, but against the very principle of education. Avant-garde culture has disfigured innovation so badly that we have to look to economic life to see why our world of internal mediation is so innovative.

Economic life is an example of an *internal mediation* that produces an enormous, even a frightening amount of innovation, since it ritualizes and institutionalizes mimetic rivalry, the rules of which are willingly obeyed. Economic agents *openly* imitate their successful rivals instead of pretending otherwise.

False as they are, the theories that dominate our cultural life are "true" in that they truly influence the cultural environment. In the arts, the scorched-earth policies of the recent past have led to a world in which radical innovation is so free to flourish that there is little difference between having it everywhere and having it nowhere at all.

The dazzling achievements of modern art and modern literature seem to give the lie to what I have just said. And it is true, indeed, that, in these domains, spiritual *autarkie* has a fecundity which has no parallel in science, technology, or economic life. Romantic and post-romantic literature thrive for a while on a diet of antiheroes and on critical or naïve portrayals of individual reactions to the pressures of internal mediation – the retreat of the modern "consciousness" into "itself".

Rousseau was the first great explorer of a territory that already had a large population when he began to write. In no time at all, he became immensely popular and had countless imitators. He ruled over the *underground* realm whose most lucid master is probably Dostoevsky. The Russian novelist's greatest work is a prodigious satire of self-pity, a luxury that much of the world cannot afford. From Rousseau to Kafka and beyond, the best of modern literature focused on the *fausse conscience* to which intellectuals are more prone than other people because of their preoccupation with those purely individual pursuits – books and works of art – that become the principal yardsticks of their being. The private question of being seems entirely separate from another and supposedly minor one – the question of where these artists and thinkers stand in relation to each other. However, in reality, the two questions are one.

CONCLUSION

After providing a great deal of genuinely innovative material, and postponing for more than a century the day of reckoning with our solipsistic ideologies, the rich vein of failed spiritual *autarkie* has finally run out, and the future of art and literature is in doubt.

Most people still try to convince themselves that our "arts and humanities" will remain forever "creative" and "innovative", fuelled by "individualism", but even the most enthusiastic espousers of recent trends are beginning to wonder. Innovation is still around, they say, but its pace is slackening.

This pessimism, which I share, is a subjective judgment – but, in such matters, can there be any other? It seems obvious to me that the still genuinely innovative areas of our culture are those in which innovation is acknowledged in modest and prudent terms, whereas those areas in which "innovation" is absolute and arrogant hide their disarray behind meaningless agitation.

I do not say this because I believe in an intrinsic superiority of the still innovative areas in our culture-science, technology, and the economy. But I think that our cultural activities are vulnerable in direct proportion to the spiritual greatness that should be theirs. The old scholastic adage always applies: *Corruptio optimi pessima* – the corruption of the best is the worst.

The true Romantics believed that if we gave up imitation entirely, deep in our selves an inexhaustible source of "creativity" would spring up, and we would produce masterpieces without having to learn anything. Mistaking the end of transcendental models for an end of *all* imitation, the Romantics and their modern successors have turned the "creative process" into a veritable theology of the self – with roots in the distant past, as we have seen. In the old dispensation, innovation was reserved for God and therefore forbidden to man. When man took upon himself the attributes of God, he became the absolute innovator.

The Latin word *innovare* implies limited change rather than total revolution – a combination of continuity and discontinuity. We have seen that, from the beginning, in the West, *innovation* departed from its Latin meaning in favour of the more "radical" view demanded by the extremes of execration and adulation alternately triggered by the idea of change.

The mimetic model of innovation is valid not only for our economic life, but for all cultural activities whose innovative potential depends on the kind of passionate imitation that derives from religious ritual and still partakes of its spirit.

Real change can only take root when it springs from the type of coherence that tradition alone provides. Tradition can only be successfully challenged from the inside. The main prerequisite for real innovation is a minimal respect for the past and a mastery of its achievements, that is, *mimesis*. To expect novelty to cleanse itself of imitation is to expect a plant to grow with its roots up in the air. In the long run, the obligation always to rebel may be more destructive of novelty than the obligation never to rebel.

But is not all this ancient history? Has not the modern theology of the self been fully discredited and discarded along with the rest of "Western metaphysics"? As the deconstruction of our philosophical tradition proceeds, shall we not be "liberated" at long last, and will not a new culture automatically flourish?

The blurring of all aesthetic and intellectual criteria of judgment underlies what is now called the "post-modern" aesthetics. This blurring parallels the elimination of truth in post-Heideggerian philosophy. Our age tries to overcome the modern obsession with the "new" through an orgy of casual imitation, an indiscriminate adoption of all models. There is no such thing anymore as a mediocre lover, in the sense of Radiguet. Pierre Menard's perfect copy of Don Quixote is just as great as the novel of Cervantes. Imitation has lost its stigma.

Does it mean that concrete innovation is back? Before we become too hopeful, we must observe that *mimesis* returns to us in a parodic and derisive mode that is a far cry from the patient, pious, and single-minded imitation of the past. The imitation that produced miracles of innovation was still obscurely related to the *mimesis* of religious ritual.

The real purpose of post-modern thinking may well be to silence, once and for all, the question that has never ceased to bedevil "creators" in our democratic world – the question of "Who is innovative and who is not?" If such is the case, post-modernism is only the latest modality of our romantic "false consciousness", one more twist of the old serpent. There will be more.

i. This text was published in English in René Girard, *Mimesis and Theory, Essays on Literature and Criticism*, 1953-2005, Robert Doran Ed., Stanford University Press, 2008.

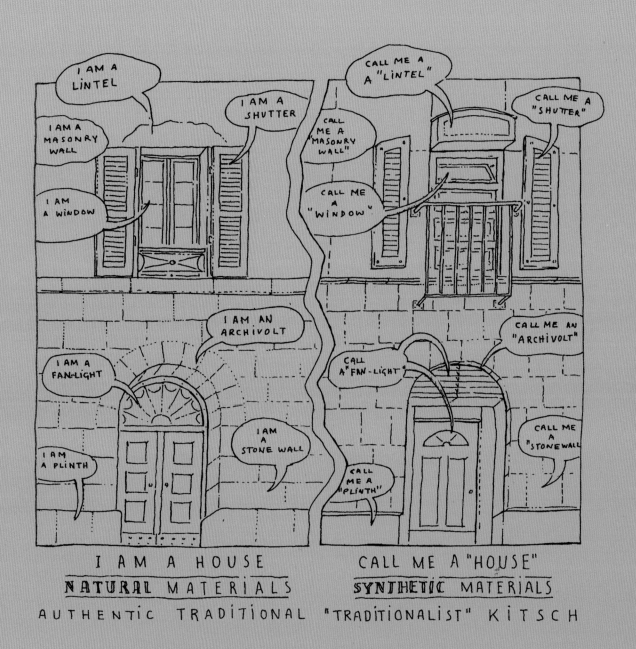

I am a house. Call me a house. Drawing by Léon Krier.

Imitation,
Hidden or Declared

Léon Krier

Vivienne Westwood, a renowned British fashion designer declared, irony not intended: "I have not been influenced by anyone but by myself, I am the Chanel of my generation." James Stirling in an interview for the *RIBA journal* famously said: "I am not influenced by individuals but by events like Cape Canaveral", implying that the Cape Kennedy launching pads are not produced by individual designers, but by impersonal forces. In the same spirit a young French designer conceded, "I am my only inspiration". And to surpass them all, Frank Lloyd Wright conceded: "Now I am the only true innovator left", when discovering during a pupil's musical recital that his only true rival for unsurpassed genius, J.S. Bach, had clearly been influenced by Vivaldi.

The refusal to own up to influences and precedents, on one hand, and the will to be influential and be considered as precedent, on the other, are evident but surprisingly little considered corollaries. Miming, imitating, and copying, are fundamental principles of nature, of life, of reproduction and hence of education and culture. Literally everthing we do or think is imitative, [and] can be ordered in mimetic patterns. This holds equally true for the mentally sane or the deranged. We are in an unprecedented situation of artists, teachers, even national educational and cultural policies denying the very foundations of their existence and raison d'être. Not only is this form of "creationism" spreading like a virus in official circles, [but] the denial of evidence doesn't cause due scandal. In an ironic twist, it becomes in turn a model of reference and hence of imitation, reproduction and copy. The head of Rome's office of *beni culturali* refused to even discuss my project for the Piazza G. Marconi in the EUR quarter, letting me know, via subordinate channels, that "the Krier project is mimetic", "it must not be mimetic", justifying her stance with a mere, "it's the law, and I am not prepared to discuss it".

The good lady is obviously unaware that a law can only be obeyed and respected via mimetic behaviour. She herself approves Richard Meier miming Le Corbusier but will not consider a project working in the spirit of the Piazza Marconi's original architectural conception, its scale, forms, materials and character.

For several decades now artists and designers are called and call themselves "creators". Now that the Gods are in extinction, would-be-gods are multiplying to fill the void. For centuries craftsmen built houses which looked like houses, with doors, windows and chimneys looking like doors, windows and chimneys. Architects equally designed temples and palaces looking like temples and palaces. Young people would apprentice with older masters and not be embarrassed to pay homage to those from whom they learned. The system still works in parenting, in manufacturing, in the military, in sports, instrument teaching, science laboratories, flying schools. It no longer seems to apply in the arts or in architecture. Starting in art schools in the late 1960s, the refusal has lately even spread to Kindergarten and elementary school teaching. How can such a state of affairs have developed? How can fantastical negations of existential realities reach dominance in cultural and educational governance?

The pretence of creating artistic or architectural works *ex nihilo*, without reference to precedent is a form of psychological derangement. It may also, in a more banal way, be a form of promotional propaganda. Factually, it is fraudulent. The sources of influence, whether denied or ignored, demonstrably exist. They are recognized by the educated mind or reconstructed by inquiry. Even for revolutionary scientific or artistic works, precedents can be traced in the whole and the detail. The quality of such works lies not in their unprecedentedness, but in the way influences are mastered and moulded with a personal touch, to the point of giving an impression of the unseen, of the never-been. Stunning newness is a characteristic of life itself. The breathtaking originality of a newborn is quite simply a demonstration of the admirable capacities of genetic codes and, for lack of a better word, of the miracle of life.

Denial of artistic or intellectual indebtedness has many explanations. When the cult of the ancients becomes tyrannical it leads to an inter-generational, an unresolvable rivalry with the dead, to revolt and wholesale irrational forms of suppression, denial and rejection. Rather than trying to surpass the unsurpassable, the wish to start afresh becomes preponderant. Do one's own thing and not care about the intelligence and brilliance of forebears, teachers, culture. Not only negligence but the obsessive cult of excellence, regularly provokes the collapse of empires, of art forms, of skills, of belief systems. What if every child plays Beethoven to perfection? Is it an enrichment of life or is it a psychological and cultural end situation? The cult of peaks and the cultivation of plains must go hand in hand.

But it is not the stance of individuals which must interest us here, but how an entire cultural system has driven itself literally into an impasse. Modernism and its post-modernist branches represent a state of crisis in the cultural reproduction system whose causes are not well understood nor quite understandable because we ourselves are an integral part of the mindset, consciously or not. The crisis was well underway when, in the nineteenth century, large country-houses were designed to look like medieval cathedrals and industrial facilities would imitate the appearance of temples and mosques. The imitative system, instead of reproducing according to type and character, initiated a massive cycle of fakes. Modernism continued the cycle, no longer faking traditional styles, typologies, and tectonics, but imitating models from outside the architectural wonder-chest, drawing inspiration from engineering works, from machine construction, from train, boat and aeroplane design. But despite the declared intentions of the would-be pioneers, stream-lining, stripping and cloning produced no serious architectural novelty, it merely poduced surrogate real-estate without architecture. After a period of kitsch and stylistic void, a return to the traditional disciplines had been formulated by Ruskin, Morris, Schmitthenner, Doyen and Hubrecht, Tessenow and others. Yet a more powerful, unchallengeable force was at work. It was in fact not its excess, but the encyclopedic treasury of tradition itself, which became the scapegoat worldwide.

The overwhelming desire for novelty, which so dominates all forms of modernism, is in fact not a desire for the unknown, but a longing to be freed from the familiar and the known, which for mysterious reasons has become disenchanted and unbearable. This desire is so powerful, that even unsurpassably beautiful cities and landscapes are sacrificed worldwide. The collective trend has transformed the desire for architecture and communality itself. We have here a clinical case for what René Girard calls metaphysical desire, i.e. a desire detached from its organic causality, architecture detached from its ancestral purpose and intelligence. A glass-house in the Sahara, at whatever cost... a factory-produce tear in your diamond-studded blue jeans and such like.

The phenomenon has morbid consequences for humans and their environs. Once the trend is initiated it is unreformable by reason, blind to its own catastrophic environmental and social consequences, building the wrong kind of buildings, in the wrong scale, materials, quantity and locations. The catastrophic failures of modernism have not led to effective reforms nor to a return to traditons but instead to a panoply of deconstructing modernisms, for that is what post-modernisms truly stands for. Miming inappropriately almost any conceivable shapes from the mineral and organic world, under the false pretence of innovation, replicating any objects, scales and situations, except those of traditonal architecture, urbanism and technology. The physical properties of reinforced synthetic materials and their fitting techniques allow at a considerable energetic cost, to imitate almost any conceivable and unsuited shape to stand up and be used as shelter, be they cloud formations, entrails, soap bubbles, bird nests, building-wrecks, eroded rock formations, crashed aeroplanes, casual stockpiles of containers.

All art and artisan teaching was, is, and will forever be based on the principle of imitation. The transmission of ideas and skills is ensured through apprenticing body and mind. It is through mimesis that the human brain is formed. Individual talent and vocation are revealed and matured through regular repetition. Indeed they cannot be identified by psychological aptitude tests alone. This is where the professional orientation of adolescence has been on the wrong track for several generations. Aristotle insisted on

the fact that the division into traditional crafts is less a result of economic human needs but more importantly of human gifts. It is the diversity of vocations which leads to the development of the different crafts. Everyone knows from experience how satisfying it is to do things one is good at and how horrendously frustrating it is to be forced to do something you have no talent for.

Desire and capacity are not always perfectly tuned, but interest and application can correct a modest skill and lead to fulfilling performance. It is here that the industrial division of human activities has caused the greatest and most lasting damage to the human condition. No amount of consumption and leisure activities can compensate for that loss. No reconstruction of a rational form of society can be successfully undertaken without addressing the issue of individual talent and forms of human occupation and production.

Drawings by Léon Krier. ABOVE: *Type & Model*. TOP RIGHT: *Mimicry*. BOTTOM RIGHT: *Master and Pupil*.

MIMICRY

creative or slavish

	model (message)	
I love		I love

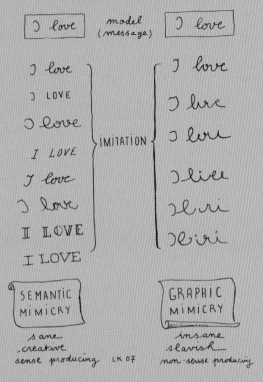

SEMANTIC MIMICRY	IMITATION	GRAPHIC MIMICRY

sane		insane
creative		slavish
sense producing	LK 07	non-sense producing

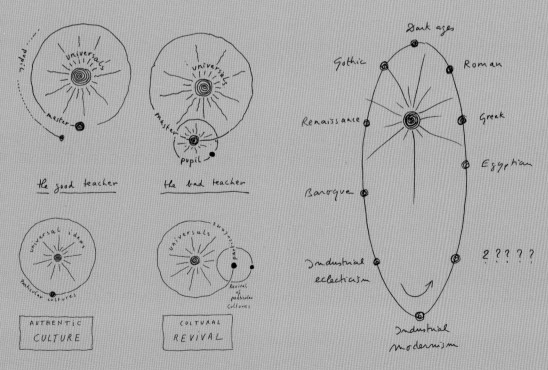

the good teacher   the bad teacher

AUTHENTIC CULTURE   CULTURAL REVIVAL

Dark ages — Gothic — Roman — Renaissance — Greek — Egyptian — Baroque — Industrial eclecticism — Industrial Modernism — ? ? ? ? ?

"We find peace near our idols." [i]

René Girard

"Aesthetic intensity offers an equivalent of war by providing an obdurate enemy –the image, the material, the ideal – to attack, subdue, and convert." [ii]

James Hillman

"We are all brothers, but it is difficult to establish who is Cain and who is Abel." [iii]

Enzo Biagi

The Other Side
of Imitation

Samir Younés

Mimesis: the Boy and the Castle. Photo Norman Crowe.

D esire for visual form, for its aesthetic appreciation, for its possession, is a characteristic shared by all. Artists and architects distinguish themselves from others in that in addition to desiring form, they have the ability to make form. Furthermore, architects distinguish themselves from artists in that the architectural ways of making are to a large extent ways of dwelling. Because we desire form, we imitate preferred forms and we also imitate the ways of making of an admired figure whom we take as a master, a model. Humans are imitative beings; from children's early imitation of their parents' actions or verbal manners, to writers imitating the prose of an exemplary literary figure, to artists and architects imitating the formal elaborations of those whose work they consider exemplary. Imitation moulds the student because it moulded the teacher and the teacher's own models. It participates in the making of tradition, the *sensus communis*. The influence of imitation extends at once to the form-making capacities of artists and architects as well as to the sculpting of their aesthetic personalities.

Santa Maria della Pace. Photo Samir Younés.

To express it differently, imitation is of two kinds: formal and personal. Architectural forms are composed by combining other architectural forms (architectural imitation), and architectural identities are composed by combining parts of the identities of other architects (personal imitation). Desire also links the possession of forms with the identity of the possessor. It is with possessiveness, with strong personal association with forms as well as the ideologies that justify them that architects sculpt their identities – a sculpting that is deeply mimetic. As we shall see, this imitation of preferred masters and forms, whereas natural to artists or architects, is also at the root of their conflicts, their antagonisms, their rivalries. When

imitation, the personal identification with form, and the claim for exclusive ownership of form converge, we have intense rivalry. It includes the rivalry amongst individuals and groups who claim the same forms, and certainly the rivalry between individuals and groups who adhere to opposing ideologies. These elements are well known to observers of the psychology of architects or artists, but what is less known is that these elements in their aggregate belong to a wider phenomenon that René Girard called: mimetic rivalry. Rarely have the effects of mimetic rivalry been considered by architects, artists, historians, and all who are concerned with the aesthetic life of the mind, for two important reasons. Imitation is either dismissed as inapplicable to present practice, or its conflictual or problematic side is unrecognized. Imitation, we said, is of two kinds: formal and personal, but it has two values, two valences: the one is beneficial, the other adverse. This phenomenon explains why, on the one hand, architects have a double mimetic relationship to each other and to their buildings; and, on the other, why they suffer deep divisions, conflicts and antagonism.

Conflicts among architects are usually explained on the basis of opposing ideologies or on the basis of contesting personalities. Ideological conflicts are often better understood because they can be justified based on a set of criteria. Conflicts based on personalities, however, are explained-away as "just quarrelling personalities", as "just colliding egos". By explaining away conflicts as just personalities, just egos, many formative elements of the psychology of architects are thereby overlooked. Indeed the very ways in which architects found their identities and form their psychologies are thus neglected or ignored.

Here is the thesis: a foundational aspect of the architect's psychology is desire for form. Imitation, or imitative inclinations are generated by this desire. Once forms are learned, once they are appropriated through mimesis, architects come to identify their personae with these forms; and this identification, this amalgamation of the persona with the form, is at the basis of their conflicts as well as their antagonisms. To put it differently, many architects conflate *to make* with *to be*. They allow little distance between their form-making capacities and their mode of being, their identities. The architect's cogito might very well be rendered as: I build, therefore I am. But it can also be extended to say: what I build is part of me. When architects justify their buildings, they justify their personae, their individual *maniere*. To will, to see, and to make thus become an indivisible psychological reality. They become aligned with the architect's image-making faculty.

Garden at Palazzo Farnese, Caprarola. Photo Samir Younés.

View of Campo Marzio, looking towards the Vatican, Rome. Photo Samir Younés.

The architects' attachment to form frequently becomes a kind of ownership of forms, or images, because architects themselves appropriate the world as an image, as a set of images. Beyond being a mere possessive quality, this attachment often becomes a potent personal identification with their forms and images and the setting in which they have been realized. Architects also dwell in and with form by surrounding themselves with desired forms, by historicizing their forms in alluring narratives, and by identifying their selves with these forms and narratives. A rich imagery fills the daily life of the architect – an aesthetic life that demands daily satisfaction. Architects enjoy surrounding themselves with images and objects that they find pleasing: fragments of entablatures, sculptures, paintings of

cityscapes and landscapes, vases, urns, candelabras, tapestries, mosaics, etc.. In short, architects develop their own personal museums.[iv] Part of this collecting derives from the accumulation of images for the uses of practical reason in composing new buildings; while another part stems from the unadulterated aesthetic pleasure of observing objects for their own sake.

Visual perception insistently participates in the formation of desire, and architectural taste is a consummate aesthetic elaboration of visual perception.[v] Taste, after all, belongs to those who desire. It results from the inward cultivation of desire based on one's subjective inclinations in relation to the subjectivities of other individuals, and in relation to group inter-subjectivity. The fascinating power of the image and the insatiable 'appetite of the eye' – in Jacques Lacan's words – induce aesthetic beings, especially architects and artists, to surpass mere participation in a perpetual exchange of desired objects toward an active construction of orders or systems of desire. In this sense, the history of architectural form, especially the kind of history with stylistic underpinnings, might rightly take its place within a larger history of desire for form. In other words, artistic and architectural history, and of course theory, can be seen as ordered constructions based on desire.

When architects imagine and draw a building, or draw forth the building, they realize the satisfaction of the conceptualizer, the painter. This satisfaction is in anticipation of realization. It is a partially fulfilled desire. The other part comes after the building is completed. This desire is teleological. But if the building is not completed to the intentions of the architect, there is frustration. The teleology is interrupted, the satisfaction only partial, and desire has to be modified to fit the incompleteness of desire. Qualities and forms that have not been realized in one building are now projected, or fantasized, onto

Gallery with Views of Modern Rome, 1759 (oil on canvas), Giovanni Paolo Pannini/ Louvre, Paris, France / Giraudon / The Bridgeman Art Library.

Hercules and Cacus, Michelangelo Buonarroti (terracotta) /
Casa Buonarroti, Florence, Italy / The Bridgeman Art Library.

entry to Piazza San Pietro in the Vatican had the Borgo not been destroyed in the early 1930s. The physical perseverance of buildings in various degrees of completion, and the mnemonic perseverance of buildings that no longer exist exert a powerful influence on the architects' imagining faculties.

Architects harbour belongings to cities, to landscapes, to an architectural tradition. As language is identity-forming so are forms and images; and this phenomenon is strikingly evident amongst the protagonists of visual culture. Architects exert much thought and passion in order to establish their identities as image-makers. With the help of historians, they remember the stories of their predecessors – the kind of psychological phenomenon that James Hillman would characterize as their attempts to "find themselves and found themselves", inscribing themselves in a story that they can claim as theirs, as in the images of a mythologized narrative. Some look at their past work with nostalgia, while others classify their life work into distinct periods ('pre' and 'post') in order to explain that the changes in their architectural expressions followed a gradual evolution ascending toward an eminent dénouement. This need to historicize their personal work, illustrates the architects' repeated attachment to and detachment from the forms that they make available to their consciousness as makers and as dwellers.

This identity-attachment has an immense scope, and ranges from attaching one's name to an architectural tradition, to a style or manner, and even to the act

the next building, as the architect's mind begins to project future formal combinations. Fantasy becomes a bridge between desire, the architect's imaging faculties, as well as an anticipated experience of satisfaction. This is why architects look forward to their next building in order to realize more of the forms that inhabit their minds. They also wonder about the forms that could have been realized by other architects. They lament the incompletion of a building which could have been a masterpiece, or the destruction of buildings that resulted in a less worthy urban condition. That is what makes architects invoke the 'original intention' of Raphael in his Villa Madama, had it been completed, or the of attaching one's name physically to a building. For example, while undertaking the archaeological work for his *envoi* from Rome, French architect Léon Vaudoyer (1785) sought to make his name endure by carving it on the Ionic arcade of the Theatre of Marcellus. Here, narcissistic naming merged personal identity, with a tradition of forms. More recently, the autograph of American architect Richard Meier was incised on the parapet wall of his pavilion to house the Ara Pacis, the altar to Augustan peace. Here, the authorship of form becomes a narcissistic identification with form. Michelangelo and Le Corbusier offer two opposing attitudes in this respect. The first, systematically destroyed his preparatory drawings, while the second was an obsessive archivist of even his most minor drawing studies.

Floating within the relativist flux of modern society are clusters of ideologies replete with their aesthetic predilections, hierarchical arrangements, disputes, and tribal alliances. In effect, architectural

Theatre of Marcellus, incision by Léon Vaudoyer, Rome. Photo Samir Younés.

ideological antagonisms may be characterized by a kind of nationalism where architects defend their positions on the ramparts of their ego-centric city. As in war, architectural antagonisms have their provocations, battlefields, entrenched camps, avant-gardes, arrière-gardes, strategists, demagogues, priestly castes, soldiers, deserters, and scapegoats. They also have their aggression, wounds, sacrifice, victories, defeats, and intermittent periods of lull. This is the often-noted martial aspect of architectural ideological antagonisms, exemplified especially in the confrontational form of debates.[vi] The image-maker becomes the image-slayer. The real for architects is the imagistically real. The image is at once the subject of their lives, their identities, the subject of their conflicts, and the material with which their conflicts are disputed.

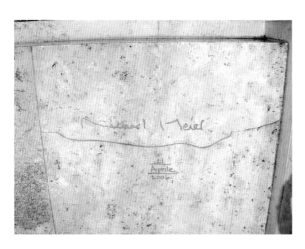

Architect's signature Ara Pacis, Rome. *Photo Samir Younés.*

Because architects are attached to their buildings as their personal acts of will, and because their attachments to their preferred buildings are insistently bound up with their narcissistic projections onto the world they build, conflicts are inherently present even before they begin architectural judgment, and even if they profess to hold no pre-conceived notions.[vii] To claim then, as some do, that architects judge without prejudice is the worst prejudice of all. Whether in debates, in architectural jury rooms, or in critical writings, architectural conflicts usually begin with a patriotic extolling of each side's architectural theory. Such exchanges usually confirm identities, but they do so through provocation and incitement.[viii] Not surprisingly, an architectural identity might be discovered precisely because of opposition to the forms architects hold dear.

Unique Forms of Continuity in Space, 1913 (bronze), Umberto Boccioni / Mattioli Collection, Milan, Italy / The Bridgeman Art Library.

Identity, conflict, and antagonism begin early in the architects' careers as students. In fact, it is in architectural schools where identity and conflict are initially incited into activity by criticism and mimetic rivalry presented as educational methods. The critical culture of the Salon, of which the architectural jury room is the raucous descendent, had already paved the way to these contentious engagements. The will and ability of the architect, as a free rational agent, to make a building in one manner also implies the power, the choice to have made this building in a different manner. Criticism moves within the space available between the different possibilities of choice. It emerges from reflections about the freedom to build based on a will, and the power to realize buildings. Consequently, criticism stems from an internal struggle between what architects expect and what they actually see. The more of their desired projects and projections are realized, the less critical they become. It follows that criticism as judgment is tenaciously tied to desire.

When the notion of architecture as an expression of a collective will-to-make and will-to-dwell in nature and the city came to be replaced with the notion of architecture as a strictly subjective representation, architects multiplied their palaces of desire. Architects exalt the power of their desires, arriving at times to a kind of idolatry. In fact they engage in a double idolatry, by idolizing the work of a chosen master or model, and by idolizing this master or model as a persona. Much of this desire relates to their double imitative relationship to each other and to their buildings, recalling our earlier note of the architect's merging between making and being. Aesthetic culture, since the commentaries of Plato and Aristotle's *Poetics* passing through the imitative theory developed from the fifteenth through the nineteenth centuries, has treated with considerable usefulness the preeminent aspects of mimesis or imitation. To achieve excellence writers imitated the work of paradigmatic figures, painters imitated nature in her products (*natura naturata*, e.g. the human body) and in her laws (*natura naturans*, e.g. the proportional relationships between parts of the human body), while, in addition to all of these, architects also imitated natural law (e.g. proportions, tectonics) as well as the time-honoured principles of a tradition. Imitation provides the intellectual discipline for artistic formation, and the theoretical foundations which enable the artist or architect to unify the best aspects of precedents with the expressions of personal invention. Imitation is the way in which the individual learns and appropriates culture, adapts to it, and participates in it. Imitation allows for inter-subjectivity between autonomous minds, while forming a bridge between the individual and society. This is the good side of imitation.

Due acknowledgement, however, should be given to René Girard for having drawn attention to a hitherto neglected side of mimesis or imitation – a conflictual side based on desire. According to Girard, the "very substance of human relations, whatever their nature, is made of mimetism[ix]". One of the fundamental axioms of human culture, continues Girard, is desire in general and mimetic desire in particular.[x] We desire an object less for what it is, and more because we imitate someone else's desire – whom we take as a model – who makes, covets or possesses that same object.[xi] The model and the ideas for which the model stands become 'mediators' by means of which we seek to attain our goals. Contrary to Freud's object-subject duality, this relationship is triangular, for we have 1) two subjects, one of whom is a model to the other; 2) imitation; 3) the desired object.

Polyphemus Attacking Acis and Galatea, 1597-1604 (fresco, detail), Annibale Carracci/ Palazzo Farnese, Rome, Italy / The Bridgeman Art Library.

Applying a Girardian perspective to the psychology of architects – a subject not covered in his writings – mimetic desire concerns more than the desired building and it is not limited to the desiring architect. Desire for Girard resides in the model, or the mediator of our desires.[xii] In this sense, architecture itself, the architectural discourse, and the very personalities of architects are all mediating agents of architects' desires for forms. Architects not only imitate each other's works, they also mimetically desire the same buildings other architects have desired. They desire each other's desires, and this is precisely the reason for which imitation is contagious. A case in point is Lord Burlington and William Kent mimetically desiring the work of Inigo Jones, who in turn had mimetically desired the work of Andrea Palladio. Moreover, architects desire the 'same ways' of pursuing other architects' desired buildings. One could consider from this point of view some of the landmarks that have strongly marked the education of the architect for centuries. The illustrated architectural treatise, the sketches in the architect's intimate *carnet de voyage*, the *capriccio* that assembles favoured buildings in a fictive setting, and the ever-present architectural photograph, all of them fulfil admirable pedagogical purposes on account of their formative roles. All of them sustain architects' desires. More precisely, these pedagogical methods illustrate the extent to which the architect's formation is largely a mimetic appropriation of other architect's desires for forms. Moreover, architects mimetically absorb their models' non-architectural preferences. This mimetism could range from a predilection to certain kinds of music or literature, to occasionally copying the vestments or even the vocal accents of admired model-architects. Consider for example the substantial number of architects who appropriated Le Corbusier's unmistakable bow tie and thickly framed glasses. Assuming a part of the appearance in some way gives the borrower the impression of having achieved a greater fullness as an architect, acquiring the mantle and the distinguished aura of an admired figure.

While desire is mimetic, it is not always in a negative sense, nor does it necessarily lead to conflict. In fact the model might serve to focus the previously vague aspirations of the imitator, while intense desire spurs the effort to transform these vague aspirations into a clearer vision based on the model's exemplary work. The model itself can be collective or individual. It can comprise an entire architectural tradition or concern the work of one single architect. It also pertains to contemporary as well as past exemplars. One instance of a collective model is the *querelle des anciens et des modernes* with its two main protagonists François Blondel and Claude Perrault and Perrault's sense of rivalry toward the ancients. From the historical perspective of the late seventeenth century, Blondel, operating under the Renaissance definition of the classical, held the view that the ancients were unsurpassable. To the contrary, the burgeoning modern scientific outlook of Perrault, transposed into architecture, led him to believe that surpassing the ancients was indeed possible and desirable. It is possible that Perrault entertained a rivalry towards the ancients. This rivalry is mimetic because the object-model is the same, for notwithstanding their theoretical differences, Blondel and Perrault did not question classical architecture as a modern practice. When the model is individual it concerns a single architect whose formal preferences are imitated by admirers who shape their own architectural desires by desiring the same forms, and even the same architectural mannerisms. The imitator's motives can range from the simple wish for learning and betterment, to a profound existential dissatisfaction with personal architectural expression, or an outright envy of the model's talents. The model's reactions also vary. Girard borrows Gregory Bateson's notion of double-bind[xiii] in which the teacher, or the model, explicitly tells the imitator: "you can imitate me", but the teacher also tacitly says: "only you cannot surpass me". The imitated model can be flattered but he or she can also reject the imitator because the imitated model developed a sense of identity and ownership with his or her forms, which the imitator was now attempting to wrest away. It is likely that the model wishes to elicit a mixture of admiration and envy on the part of the imitator. It is even possible that the model-teacher harbours a desire to see frustration on the part of the imitator-follower who has troubled the waters into which the narcissistic model had been gazing. Tragedy is not far. In this case, the rejected follower abandons the desire to imitate *that* master, or model, while retaining the 'violence' of the rejection. Subsequently, both the model and the imitator undertake to wrest away from each other the object of their common desire. Mimetic desire now becomes mimetic rivalry, leading to mutual attempts to discredit the other, as the actions of both sides gradually increase in resemblance. Rivalry and then antagonism become unavoidable; and when mimetic rivalry turns into pure antagonism, the object of this rivalry becomes less important than personal animosity. Hostility becomes cumulative and more acute because of architects' association of their personal identity with their vocational identity. Here, criticism becomes the artistic substitute for societal violence. Criticism becomes a mimetic violence, a form of mutual psychological lapidation. When veiled under an academic robe criticism, though an offensive intellectual gesture, takes its place alongside the respectful dialogue that derives from classical humanism.[xiv]

Moreover, beyond destroying the validity of a building, one particular kind of injurious criticism also seeks to generate feelings of inadequacy, of deficiency in the criticized architect. It can also be a terrible condemnation, an excommunication of the architect's prime identity: the persona. Criticism then becomes a subversive game of mutual derision. "We criticize the faults of others", said François de La Rochefoucauld in his usual blend of wit and irony, "more out of pride than goodness; and we criticize them not so much to correct them as to persuade them that we are free from their faults." Regrettably, much architectural criticism is not necessarily offered with a constructive end in mind.

This rivalry is mimetic because it is a confluence between two sets of egotistical phenomena: the architects' personal identification with preferred forms, and their imitation of their rivals' successes in order to achieve similar success, or at least claim primacy. Mimetic rivalry often "characterizes the desire of the imitator because it already characterizes the model's desire".[xv] The fact that the imitator and the model desire the same object is no guarantee that they will enjoy an untroubled relationship. Because it revolves around architecture as the mediator of their desires, mimetic rivalry, uncomfortably demonstrates to architects that their discord is only partially attributable to ideological differences, and that some of the main causes for discord reside within themselves. And one primary reason for discord stems from architects' aggressive "thirst for exclusive possession" – in Girard's terms. Such might have been, for example, the relationship between Hadrian and Apollodorus (if one is to believe Dio Cassius), Michelangelo's maliciousness towards his rivals, the plotting regarding the commission for the extension of the Louvre between the Perrault brothers and Bernini, the acute rivalry that played out in Rome between Bernini and Borromini, and the deep animosities between the leaders of modernism.[xvi] The crisis exacerbates the desire for appropriation of forms or fame amongst mimetic rivals, and the phenomenon becomes viciously circular, being continuously fuelled by the renewed momentum of desire itself. When it migrates to the group, it can turn into what Hobbes called the "war of all against all". That is

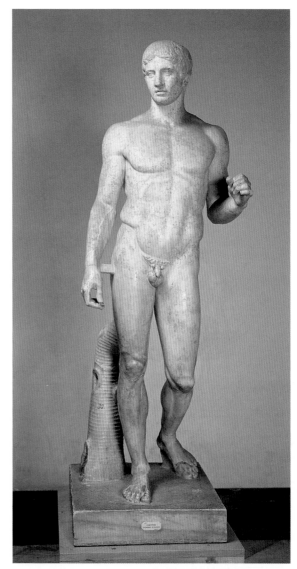

Athlete, Roman copy after an original by Polykleitos (fl.c.450-c.415 BC) in Pompeii (marble) / Museo Archeologico Nazionale, Naples, Italy / The Bridgeman Art Library.

if it remains unchecked by external forces capable of neutralizing conflicts, or diffused by the presence of an expiatory scapegoat who substitutes for the actual conflict or antagonism.[xvii] An illustration of this phenomenon was the organized collective sentencing of the classical tradition on the part of many rivaling modernist groups competing for primacy on the international architectural scene.

Next, mimetic rivals come to consider themselves as equals. They are equals who are fascinated by one another, studying each other's work carefully, and vying for the same front row position facing the collective mirror of society. This fascination, however, is rarely admitted; for, contrary to children, adults are embarrassed to admit that they model themselves on others. It is easier for architects to admit that they imitate the work of architects from the past than to admit that they imitate the work of their living contemporaries. When contemporary architects claim that they imitate no one, it is probable that they are hiding their desire to imitate in order to claim complete independence and autonomy as inventors of form. In this way they can be faithful to the myth of the modernist genius, the romantic individualist creator who invents new objects from nothing, and who walks in no one's shadow. This shows the ambiguity between architects' natural inclination to imitate an exemplar, because humans are imitative beings, and their declared self-sufficiency and claim to make new buildings *ex nihilo*, out of nothing.

When the antagonism is between groups with different ideologies, the enemy is the other, the 'stranger outside' the architectural clan. An individual's or a group's identity is confirmed by opposing the other. Exterior influences are at once excluded and seen as subordinate to the group's ideology. Evidence for this is seen in the widespread use of the language of otherness in architectural circles today, where the encounter of one ideology

Exterior view of S. Maria del Fiore, 1294-1436 (photo) / Duomo, Florence, Italy / The Bridgeman Art Library.

with another is usually employed in order to assert the pre-eminence of one over the other. Advocates of one ideology judge other ideologies by the tenets of their own while projecting the worst expectations on the other – on "them". When the antagonism is within the same group, the enemy is the 'stranger inside', vying for a higher position within a pre-established hierarchy and using a commonly held ideology as a basis for dispute. Here, even the smallest difference, or what S. Freud[xviii] called the "narcissism of small differences", becomes the justification for ideological divisions and fratricidal antagonisms among members who otherwise share the same beliefs. This is one of the reasons why movements fail. The winner achieves a temporary satisfaction in having prevailed over an architectural argument, or prevented another architect from obtaining a desired commission. Satisfaction might soon be succeeded by an empty feeling of victory, or eventually by a renewed search for yet another clash followed by another expected win. The winner might very well think that it was Mars who triumphed, whereas in all probability the victor was Cain. Regrettably, the love for architecture does not suffice to placate the odium between conflicting architects.

When architects relentlessly and frenetically uphold difference, separateness, and their intellectual auto-centric autonomy at the expense of collectively shared aims, discord becomes inevitable. And this discord is achieved irrespective of ideological commonalities or divergence. Hyper-critical difference becomes a method[xix] – a project that regards the practice of architecture as a methodological pursuit of ultra-individualism. Even inside a small group of architects who share the same ideology, the narcissism of small differences presents occasions to underline further differentiations. Small groups are then fragmented into even smaller units, leading eventually to a complete breakdown of any cohesive structure. This, again, is one of the reasons why movements fail. In sharpening their politics of difference architects frequently overlook that opposition to other architectural identities is insufficient to form an identity of their own, although as mentioned earlier, opposition and judgment provoke or incite identity. Most importantly, the insistence on personifying difference with respect to judgment, sometimes makes architects overlook a fundamental constituent of judgment, namely, the ground upon which judgment is based.

Nowhere is the architect's narcissistic determination to differ more evident than in public, in the midst of an audience. There, the architect must be understood as the illumined actor on stage, a constructed dramatic figure being at once subject and object, mediator of desire and the object of desire, exhibitionist and voyeur, judge and partisan, executioner and victim. With the charisma of theatrical postures, with the art of clichégenic statements, architects deliver their sweeping judgments, exhibiting discriminating knowledge of the most arcane subjects, displaying a wide aesthetic culture and an appreciation of different aesthetic cultures. They demonstrate sensitivity to forms, proportions, materials, colours, and expand on visions of wide ecological breadth. They know the reasons for inclining columns and curving stylobates for the purpose of eurythmic adjustments. They can expertly contrast the proportions of the Doryphoros with those of Bernini's *Apollo* and *Daphne*, while describing the different aesthetic pleasures that derive from preferring one over the other. They are sensitive to the tenebrism of Caravagio and Juan de Ribera, and the contrapuntal inventions in Johann Sebastian Bach's fugues. With gastronomical delectation they worry about the temperature of a Saint-Emilion and the necessary breathing time for a Sassicaia. They speak with great erudition of the soothing effects of an Yquem following dinner as well as the architectural additions to the

Château d'Yquem as it passed from the Sauvage d'Yquem family to the Lur Saluces family in the late eighteenth century – through marriage. They are the masters of the rarified airs of stylish exchanges in art galleries displaying their taste for multiple genres of music, literature, poetry, theatre, and film. Yet, their laboriously cultivated aesthetic lives do not suffice to restrain their angered Jupiterean gaze, their terrible penchant for discord, for petty self-absorption, unbridled self-aggrandizement, and the undervaluing of the work of other architects.[xx] They desire fame, and enjoy being applauded for their contributions to culture and the culture of building, for their creativity, their originality, and the complex reasoning they undertook in order to achieve their admirable *tour de force*. They enjoy the authority of their own reflection in the mirror and vow to seduce the mirror itself. Above all, architects are authorities on themselves.

Narcissus, c.1597-99 (oil on canvas), Caravaggio/ Palazzo Barberini, Rome, Italy / The Bridgeman Art Library.

i. Des choses cachées depuis la fondation du monde, Paris, Grasset, 1978, p. 279.

ii. A Terrible Love of War, Penguin, N.Y., 2004, p. 213.

iii. Siamo tutti fratelli, ma è difficile stabilire chi sia Caino e chi sia Abele. Author's Translation.

iv. The desire for objects of art and architecture (as well as their plunder in war) in order to include them within the confines of a single enclosure constitutes a significant basis for the development of the museum and the museal mentality. In fact the museum as a receptacle for critically selected objects of desire bears strongly on socially instituted artistic judgment. Once this phenomenon is extended to the city, it correlates with desires to conserve buildings. These desires are then formulated in conservation policies and laws.

v. Many architects discuss the pleasures of taste and its effects on all the senses. They point to analogies between architectural composition and the compositions of culinary art and its effects on seeing, smelling and tasting. Some pasticceri like Bartolomeo Scappi, the "secret cook of the popes" in sixteenth century Rome, occasionally composed architectural culinary fantasies, see, J. di Schino and F. Luccichenti, Il cuoco segreto dei Papi, Gangemi, Rome, 2007. Few are the architects or artists, however, who have taken the analogy so close as the legendary French pâtissier-architecte, Antonin Carême. Carême produced his culinary compositions based on diligent architectural studies of the treatises of Vignola, Palladio, Durand, Ledoux, as well as architectural travel books such as those of Alexandre de la Borde, and architectural descriptive texts such as those of Krafft and Ransonnette. Seeing architecture and cooking as fine arts, he even proposed several architectural schemes for the embellishment of Paris and Saint Petersburg. He designed a project for a triumphal column in the Place du Carrousel, presented proposals for the completion of the bridge of the Concorde, a triumphal arch for L'Etoile, and an idea for a new Opéra de Paris. Of his voluminous works, the most important for architecture is Le Pâtissier pittoresque, précédé d'un traité des cinq ordres d'architecture (1828), and parts of his posthumous five volume L'Art de la cuisine française au XIXème siècle, (1833-44), Payot-Rivages, 1994. Georges Bernier's study A. Carême (1783-1833). La sensibilité gourmande en Europe, Grasset, 1989, discusses Carême's influence on the 'culinary revolution' in late eighteenth century Europe.

vi. This parallels F. Nietzsche's notion of will to power, developed in his Beyond Good and Evil and The Will to Power – the view that all human relations may be interpreted in terms of power relationships intending on expanding their sphere of influence.

vii. See Carl Jung's discussion of the psychology of projections in The Essential Jung, Anthony Storr, Ed., Princeton University Press, 1983, pp. 87-125.

viii. On identity and incitement, see Amin Maalouf, Les identités meurtrières, Grasset, 1998.

ix. "La substance même des rapports humains, quels qu'ils soient, est faite de mimétisme." Girard, Celui par qui le scandale arrive, p.8. Author's translation. Girard's reflections meet Lacan's conclusions that "man's desire is the desire of the other". See Lacan's "Of the Gaze as objet petit A", in The Continental Aesthetics Reader, Clive Cazeaux, Ed., Routledge, 2000, p. 540.

x. The notion of mimetic desire, mimetic rivalry and violence, is developed in René Girard's La violence et le sacré, (1972), Pluriel, 1990, especially chapter VI, "Du désir mimétique au double monstrueux", pp.213-249; Des choses

cachées depuis la fondation du monde, Grasset, 1978; To Double Business Bound, Johns Hopkins, 1978; Celui par qui le scandale arrive, Desclée de Brouwer, 2001; La voix méconnue du réel, Grasset, 2002; The Girard Reader, James Williams, Ed., Crossroads Herder, 2003, especially pp. 9-62; Les origines de la culture, Pluriel, 2004; and Politiques de Caïn, Domenica Mazzù, Ed., Desclée de Brouwer, 2004.

xi. The words mimesis and imitation are used here in their most elementary sense of 'making like', and not in the artistic sense of imitating nature, imitating the principles of a tradition, or stone imitating wood, etc..

xii. R. Girard's "Les appartenances", in Politiques de Caïn, pp.19-33.

xiii. Gregory Bateson, "Double bind", in Steps to an Ecology of the Mind, New York: Ballantine, 1969-72, pp. 271-278.

xiv. The phenomenon of "mean thought" has been surveyed in two recent studies: Vincent Azoulay & Patrick Boucheron, Le mot qui tue. Une histoire des violences intellectuelles de l'antiquité à nos jours, Champ Vallon, 2009; and Pierre Drachline, Ed. Le grand livre de la méchanceté, J'ai lu, 2009.

xv. Girard, Politiques…, p. 24. Author's translation.

xvi. Michelangelo's denouncement of Baccio d'Agnolo's arcaded loggia that was to surround the octagonal drum of Santa Maria del Fiore in Florence as a 'cricket cage', sufficed to halt the construction of the project. The famous rivalry between Bernini and Borromini has been recently retold and elaborated in Jake Morrissey's The Genius in the Design, Duckworth, U.K. 2005, and Nick Mileti's Beyond Michelangelo, Xlibris, N.J., 2005. Rudolf and Margot Wittkower's study, Born Under Saturn, Norton, 1963, of the professional rivalries, jealousies, and ambitions of artists from antiquity until the 18th century remains a useful source. For an account of the rivalry amongst figures of modernism see Tom Wolfe, From Bauhaus to our House, Farrar Straus Giroux, N.Y., 1981.

xvii. Girard called this phenomenon, the "victimizing mechanism" in Des choses cachées…, chap.3. The scapegoat closes Girard's notion of the fourfold mimetic mechanism: it begins with mimetic desire, develops into mimetic rivalry, becomes exasperated by a mimetic crisis that eventually necessitates some kind of sacrifice – a scapegoat. Origines de la culture, Pluriel, 2004, pp. 61-102.

xviii. Sigmund Freud, Moïse et le monothéisme, (1939), Gallimard, 1967. On the stranger from without and within, see Julia Kristeva, Etrangers à nous mêmes, Paris, Gallimard, 1991, and Georg Simmel, Sociologie, études sur les formes de la socialisation, Paris, P.U.F., 1999.

xix. This may, but does not necessarily lead to J. Derrida's différance – his intentional misspelling of the French word différence as a punning play on the verb différer which can be rendered in English as to differ or defer. J. Derrida, Speech and Phenomena and Other Essays on Husserl's Theory of Signs. D. Allison Tr., Evanston, Ill. 1973.

xx. The culture of self-inflation has been clearly examined in Christopher Lasch, Culture of Narcissism, Norton, 1991, Richard Sennett, The Fall of Public Man, Norton, 1992, and Ken Wilber, Boomeritis, Shambhala, 2002.

Stone graining. Drawing by Kent Bloomer.

The Sacrifice of Ornament in the Twentieth Century

Kent Bloomer

INTRODUCTION

An ideological rivalry between proponents and opponents of ornament in architecture coincided with the modernist critique of classicism in the early twentieth century. While the term "function" would have historically included cultural functions in the light of decorum, cosmos, social organization . . . , the emerging new canon limited function's conventional meaning in architecture to rational indices such as industrial standardization and plan efficiency.

Shortly after World War II, Western schools of design overwhelmingly adopted the modernist ideology and as a consequence ornament, no longer just a controversy, was eliminated from their core curriculums and its practice came to be regarded as deviant. Could ornament, personified, be considered a scapegoat in a larger, perhaps unconscious conflict that was simmering in the twentieth-century Academies of Art and Architecture?

THE OMISSION

When I was a student of architecture, about a half-century ago, something happened during a lecture on what was referred to as "progressive architecture". I have never forgotten that moment which, over time, had such a great import on the conduct of my practice within the visual arts and architecture. I cannot recall the exact words, but it went something like this. The professor projected an image of the Carson Pirie Scott, originally the Schlesinger & Mayer, Department Store in Chicago, completed in 1906. Almost immediately he shifted the angle of projection to cut off the two-story

Carson Pirie Scott Building, Louis Sullivan, 1899, Chicago. National Register of Historic Places.

term "modernism" came to be associated with actual progress. Keep in mind that ornament had been a property of architecture for an untold thousand of years, basically forever. Not only was the study omitted, most discussion of ornament was clouded or avoided by a stridently pejorative attitude, as though a taboo existed. There was both a contempt and a fear of ornament. I began years ago to suspect there must be an explanation, perhaps a malaise, that lurked behind the academic discourse on ornament, or perhaps we should say the destruction of that discourse in schools of art and architecture. That suspicion was fuelled by the absence of a single credible (rational, aesthetic, or pragmatic) explanation for deploring the practice of such an enormous legacy. Let me mention some of the bizarre explanations uttered in the early years of the modern movement and nicely assembled by Mark Wigley in his work *White Walls and Designer Dresses.*

base declaring it was best not to look down there. From the third floor upward we were to observe how architecture had progressed and to take note of its elegant regularity and whiteness. My curiosity was aroused. Why was there such a move to shield something? A few of us rushed off to the library and discovered the extraordinary ornament of Louis Sullivan which had evidently been removed from view for being 'not progressive'.

The complete omission, indeed the cancellation, of the study of ornament from the core curriculum of education in architecture became official in the second half of the twentieth century. Its absence became an accepted article of modernism and the

- Ornament was unclean, an uncleanliness that fouled clean design.
- In fact, it was a prostitution, a sexual lure and seduction. It was effeminate and deviant.

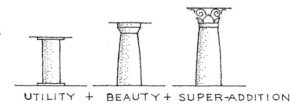

UTILITY + BEAUTY + SUPER-ADDITION

Utility-added-super-added. Drawing by Kent Bloomer.

Carson Pirie Scott Building, Entrance, Louis Sullivan, 1899, Chicago. Photo Beyond My Ken, Wikimedia Commons.

- Performing as inessential surplus, it masked the truth and thus it was a lie, a cover-up.
- And then there was Loos's intentional (or accidental) criminalization of ornament: "A CRIME"!

Samir Younés's mention of mimetic rivalry struck a chord. Reading René Girard's notions of rivalry, sacrifice, and victim seemed to provide clues, perhaps even the explanation for a procedure in which the practice of ornament was first vilified, then indicted and finally condemned. Could it be that the study and practice of ornament was indicted and then sacrificed? Was ornament personified made a scapegoat in the effort to resolve some sort of rivalry; but if so, between whom and for what? My thesis will assume that ornament was capable of addressing (perhaps even resolving) one of the most vexing problems of the twentieth century, a problem that the professional academies of art and architecture did not want to resolve.

The unwanted problem was how, in our art and architecture, can we connect (or re-combine) the disparate pieces of an increasingly fractured and atomized vision of the world and of ourselves, pieces that appear to have been visually united in the fabric of the great buildings to which the ideal of architecture owes its profound original identity.

The exemplary and treasured models of seminal Western architecture such as the Greek Temple, the Roman Forum and Pantheon, the thirteenth-century Cathedral, the ideal Renaissance Villa, even the nineteenth and early twentieth-century Railroad Station and Library, sought to express, if only momentarily, a vision of an ordered world, a "peaceable kingdom" that revealed the 'cosmos' of life. Expressing and memorializing an ordered cosmos was the subject of civic architecture. And throughout my life it has been evident that ornament was a critical player, a *parergon*, in expressing this extraordinary and inspiring order.

But let me digress for a few paragraphs and say how I am employing the term "ornament".

Originally the Latin term "*ornamentum*" from the verb "*ornare*", to equip, meant being an accessory to a useful thing such as a bowl or a temple. The term "ornament" is a Western word, without an equivalent in ancient Greek or Chinese vocabularies, although the ancient Greek word closest to "ornament" is thought to be "cosmos". In his sixth book, *On Ornament*, Alberti declared "ornament may be defined as a form of auxiliary light and complement to beauty. From this it follows … that beauty is some inherent property to be found suffused all through the body of that which may be called beautiful; whereas ornament, rather than being inherent, has the character of something attached or additional,"[i] albeit an essential property of architecture. Ornament performs as cosmos suffusing beauty.

Leaping from the fifteenth to the mid-nineteenth century Christopher Dresser, one of England's greatest theorists, makes a similar statement. "Ornament is that which, super-added to utility, renders the object more acceptable through bestowing upon it an amount of beauty which it would not otherwise possess."[ii] Here Dresser suggests that an amount of beauty is first added to utility (such as shaping a bowl into a beautiful form) before ornament (such as foliation) is super-added to that shape to complete the project. In respect to both statements, observe that the combination of ornament and the practical thing constitutes a heterogeneous system of at least three formal agendas, i.e., the inherent utilitarian agenda, the ordering of beauty, and the incorporation of adhering auxiliaries or super-additions.

Greek amphora. Drawing by Kent Bloomer.

(The first and most fundamental principle of ornament, therefore, is that figures of ornament are dependent upon an object (the thing) being ornamented in order to perform. Figures of ornament always act in combination with other elements of design and do not aspire to be autonomous or self-sufficient.

Understanding that the objects being ornamented ordinarily have typical original and economic forms of their own, i.e. immediately recognizable shapes such as bowls and buildings, we can discern that the fundamental figures of ornament (for example spirals and zigzags) are different and originate from the world-at-large outside their object. Ornament is not merely an elaboration or an augmentation of the object's form. Consider an acanthus or a spiral expressing the organic and expansive idea of growth as distinct from the static geometry of a vessel shaped by the need to contain liquid. That combination of expansion and containment exhibits a balance in which the adherent figures of ornament remain distinct from the inherent form of the object and thereby manifest the different movements through an intimate coincidence, i.e. a consonant union of visible differences in the material body of the vessel.

(The product is neither a purée nor a synthesis in the scientific sense of two compounds producing an entirely new compound. The embedding of ornament in an object contributes to a complex visual product capable of expressing several ideas

The Triumph of Galatea, 1512-14 (fresco), Raffaello Sanzio / Villa Farnesina, Rome, Italy / Giraudon / The Bridgeman Art Library.

simultaneously with each expression remaining visually intact.

SPECIALIZATION

Returning to the notion that ornament was sacrificed, we must ask again, why would such a discriminate union of apparent dissimilarities provoke hostility in the emerging twentieth-century ideology governing modern architecture? We know that during the Enlightenment specialization evolved from the progressive compartmentalizing of learned and professional disciplines. That specialization was intensified by the growth of scientific studies. In the eighteenth century different kinds of national schools were founded. "Engineering schools emerged as independent institutions around 1740 in France and 1754 in Germany, while medical academies asserted their independence from scientific societies throughout the eighteenth century. Like industry itself, this specialization created a complex division of purposeful labour." The refinement of classical composition in architecture "had benefited from an embodied and memorable legacy when it was centered around a sacred model, but with the Enlightenment a process of disembodiment evolved."[iii]

"While the Royal Academy of Architecture in France emphasized the scientific approach to architecture, the Ecole des Beaux-Arts, founded shortly after the French Revolution, treated architecture as an art. It started with a concern for human experience, personal identity, and a carefully developed sense of compositional order and beauty."[iv]

These qualities defied (as they still do) the precise quantification found in science. A schism of sorts resulted from the two trajectories of engineering and art, both claiming to teach the fundamentals of architecture. The academies of fine art enjoyed a variety of visual 'thinkers' (as we might say today) including painters, sculptors, and architects. Although they could work separately and possessed different skills they also worked together under the muse of the fine arts, especially in the production of buildings. In Ruskin's *Seven Lamps of Architecture* it was taken for granted that painters, sculptors, and artisans were united to work within the project of architecture. The notion of architecture as the mother of the arts implied, in the late nineteenth century, that architecture held a maternal responsibility towards the other visual practices and their different ways of imagining. However, some cracks eventually appeared in the community of the fine arts that were to erupt in the twentieth century.

"Between 1750 and 1758, within the same academic climate that led to the founding of schools of art, engineering, and applied science, the German philosopher Alexander Baumgarten wrote two volumes called *Aesthetika* in which he attempted to establish aesthetics as a scientific study. His was the first systematic effort to employ rational principles and scientific rules for the treatment of the beautiful, and to elevate the study of that which depends on feelings and the sense of beauty to the status of a science with an independent body of knowledge. By recognizing that feelings dealt with sensitive knowing as compared to rational knowing, Baumgarten proposed that sensing the beautiful was *real* knowledge."[v] His conclusions, however, had the effect of taking with his left hand what he had given with his right, for he emphasized the difference between the non-rational knowledge derived from the senses and the pure knowledge derived rationally from logic, and he continued to declare that while sensible knowledge was also real knowledge, it was nevertheless inferior to the clear and distinct knowledge developed logically by the mind. Thus the science of aesthetics was dubbed by its founder to be a science of lower knowledge; art, it was implied, was inferior to science.

As the subjects of art were set apart from the scientific mainstream of higher knowledge, they were increasingly toughing it out within the halls of higher education to gain their share of respect. Their advocates declared that individual works of art were complete and definite carriers of truth in their own way. Indeed, a great work of art should be granted self-sufficiency and recognized as a work of genius that could stand alone like an elegant equation in physics.

In his preface to *Mademoiselle de Maupin*, published in 1835, the French critic and writer, Théophile Gautier, articulated the earliest expression of "Art for Art's Sake" as he attacked and degraded the bourgeois valuation of usefulness and useful work. "There is nothing truly beautiful but that which can never be of any use whatsoever."[vi] His ideas were further developed in his poem *Art*, …, published in 1857, in which he opposed the idea of art as imitation, claiming that the artist's creative imagination or 'inner vision' should be the source of inspiration.

The critic, writer, and Oxford don, Walter Pater, became the leading proponent of the Art for Art's Sake movement in England with the publication of *Studies in the History of the Renaissance* in 1873. Because music was immaterial and independent of subject matter, unlike art in which matter (subject); and form (execution), could be distinguished, Pater made his famous proclamation: "*All art constantly aspires towards the condition of music*" (his italics). He further claimed, "this form, this mode of handling, should become an end in itself … this is what all art constantly strives after." [vii] "Art, then, is always striving to be independent of mere intelligence, to become a matter of pure perception, to get rid of its responsibilities to its subject or material … [a] perfect identification of matter and form."[viii]

Works of art, Pater insisted, should express one's personal impressions rather than objective standards. The best works "bear the impress of a personal quality, a profound expressiveness … some subtler sense of originality – the seal on a man's work of what is most inward and peculiar in

Seagram Building, Mies van der Rohe, 1958, New York. Photo Dan De Luca, Creative Commons.

his moods and manner of apprehension: it is what we call *expression*, carried to its highest intensity of degree" ix (his italics). [Here we have a *call for self-expression*.] In his concluding chapter, which is considered a manifesto of the Art for Art's Sake movement in England, he emphasized the priority of experience. "Not the fruit of experience, but experience itself, is the end.... To burn always with this hard, gemlike flame, to maintain this ecstasy, is success in life." Experience had priority over theory. Life, he argued, was a continuum of fleeting impressions, every moment passing even as it was being reflected upon, hence "we shall hardly have time to make theories about the things we see and

touch. What we have to do is to be forever testing new opinions and courting new impressions, [here we have a *call for innovation*] never acquiescing in a facile orthodoxy."x [Here we have *aversion to past ideas*]. "For art comes to you proposing frankly to give nothing but the highest quality to your moments as they pass, and simply for those moments' sake."xi [Here we have a *reverence for the temporary and the hyper-present*.] His theories profoundly influenced Oscar Wilde and promoted decadent behaviour.

The nineteenth-century Art for Art's Sake movement propelled the arts to cut themselves off from the past and, like the sciences, to search instead for novelty, uniqueness, and the cutting edge. Tradition and imitation were becoming associated with contamination, with dangers to the process of creativity and newness. Ridding art of those contaminates would clarify the search for pure uncorrupted properties and would also distinguish the essential (the special) nature of each discipline belonging to the family of the arts. For example, what are the special properties belonging to painting, to sculpture, to architecture? Obviously if such properties could be found, then specific territories could be deeded to each member. The fine arts were being prepared for compartmentalization and compartmentalization would fuel territorial rivalry.

All of this was coming together at the beginning of the twentieth century as notions of modernism and progress in design were being formulated. The fine artist's production of autonomous objects had established a foothold in the great museums designed to give their works individual locations and to sanctify their ability to stand alone. The construction of particular buildings already provided with individual locations guaranteed a sense of autonomy to a work of architecture.

Around 1900 the decorative arts, which include ornament, were expelled from the museums of fine art because they depended upon and were implicated with objects such as bowls, walls, and buildings. They were not autonomous; therefore they were not sufficiently 'fine' to be elegant carriers of truth all by themselves. The distinction between fine art and applied art stiffened. The fine arts had gained a tentative foothold of equality with the sciences, at least enough so they could now claim to also express 'creative' genius. And, while scientists were already bestowed with a superior status, the fine arts would proceed to make their own claim to superiority by demoting those among them who depended upon utilitarian forms for their production such as decorators and ornamenters.

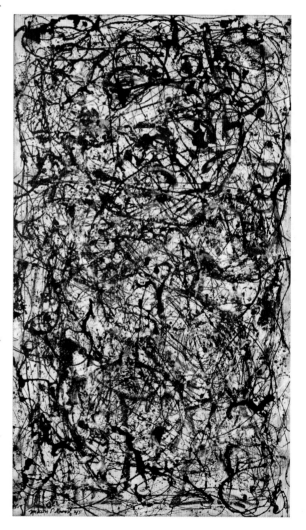

Number 26A: Black and White, 1948 (enamel on canvas), Jackson Pollock/ Musée National d'Art Moderne, Centre Pompidou, Paris, France / Giraudon / The Bridgeman Art Library.

THE RIVALRY

Already in a schism with engineering, architecture was now at odds with disciplines in the fine arts for appearing to have a leg in both fine art and the practical sciences. It more desperately needed a *pure* academic identity of its own. In 1962 the art historian Kenneth Clark wrote a provocative article titled *The Blot and the Diagram*. The Seagram Building had been completed in 1957 and Jackson Pollock's canvases typified the contemporary abstract expressionist movement in painting.

Clark observed both a similarity and dissimilarity between the works of Mies and Pollock. Both the architect and the painter engaged in a type of fine-grained compositional repetition or isotropy, a homogeneity that filled the boundaries of their compositions. The profound difference between them was that "the architecture went off in one direction with the diagram and painting went in another with the blot."[xii] He also surmised they would go well together, a Pollock in a Miesian space, with the intuitively painted blots standing for "the embers of fire, or clouds, or mud", while the diagram stood for "a rational statement in a visible form involving measurements and done with an ulterior motive."[xiii] Here we have a painter and an architect imagining the world from different viewpoints with the proposition that their work, combined together, would provide a more complete or more fulfilled world-picture.

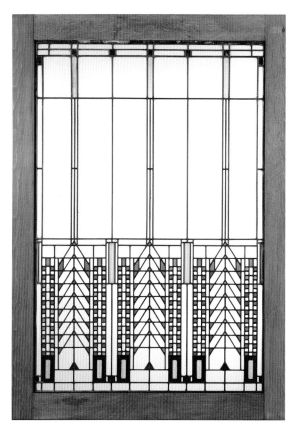

Window, 1904 (leaded glass), Frank Lloyd Wright/ Private Collection / The Bridgeman Art Library.

Yet the physical manifestation of the diagram by itself, bereft of the blot, was the essence the architects were seeking; no other modern art was better constituted to express the pure and rational ordering of concrete space than architecture. That was a clue to their province, their unique purpose, and their elusive 'self'. They could do without the "embers". Architects could manage without ornament.

In the second half of the twentieth century the academic establishment as a whole was shifting across the board from the liberal arts to professional studies. The federal government in the 1970s demanded that architectural schools provide "criterion for the criterion": for holding an exclusive claim on the use of the word "architect". Architects not only craved a stronger academic identity, they were now required to produce a professional one or they could not be recognized as a legal entity with all the attendant 'rights'. They had to specify more precisely what they were, and indirectly what they were not.

And so they did. They chose to officially purge, that is to sacrifice, those elements and traditions in architecture that might compromise or contaminate their identity as a distinct practice performing rational tasks. They emphasized that architecture had its own very special function apart from the visual arts. To perform like architects rather than artists meant, in a curious academically political way, that they had to appear to remove the seemingly unnecessary art-like features in architecture, a project that they further implemented by founding their own autonomous schools and divorcing the schools of fine art altogether, even as they continued to mimic the produce and behaviour of art and artists e.g. 'cubist' composition in the sixties and seventies and 'wiggles' towards the end of the century and today.

Because architecture was an integral part of the fine arts academy in the nineteenth century it was also implicated with the "Art for Art's Sake" movement. Its legacy, its 'self', included much of the histrionics generated within that academy's rhetoric even as it moved to segregate itself from being identified with art itself. A territorial rivalry between the 'self' of architecture and the 'self' of art was underway.

The schism with schools of engineering had become resolved by the mid-twentieth century. The licensed architect held the authority to do his own engineering as long as he carried the liability. In large projects he could sub-contract an engineer without losing his claim to be the architect and principal designer. However, the fickle affair between modern architecture and modern art became more complicated. Architecture, while mimicking certain ways of thinking associated with art, had to confirm its commitment to an identity predicated on the rational concretized diagram. The modernist Academies of Architecture had to critique those elements and traditions still lingering within the classical legacy of architecture that might, for being art-like, compromise or contaminate the logical purity of their new project. In an uncanny way the modern movement in the architecture of the late twentieth century proceeded to replay the polemics of the nineteenth-century movement of Art for Art's Sake, but this time it became an unstated 'Architecture for Architecture's Sake', although now the protagonist was claiming to be the useful and rational figure. Paradoxically architecture moved to reject the idea 'art' from its fabric even as it adopted art's nineteenth-century rhetoric. We can almost quote Walter Pater. The new architecture proceeded to strive for self-expression, i.e. the 'self' of the architect and the institutional 'self' of the new practice, to be emphatically innovative, to reject the work of the past, and to operate in the hyper-present, i.e. the contemporary. The new architect was to be a creator, and creative geniuses were not supposed to imitate.

THE PROCEDURE

The circumstances leading to the sacrifice of ornament were convoluted. Ornament, despite its brilliant surge in early twentieth century modern architecture (Sullivan, Wright, Horta), is not only art-like, albeit not 'fine-art'-like, it respects and reiterates an ancient tradition with arguably the longest history among all the visual arts.

Yet ornament's art-likeness and tradition evidently did not provide the most damning rationale to justify its sacrifice. In the formative years of modernism ornament was theoretically allowed a qualified membership in the modern project, so long as its figuration was composed exclusively from structural details, materials and spatial metrics *innate* to the tectonic ordering of space. Thus the graining of wood and stone (e.g. Looshaus or Mies's Tugendhat house) or arrays of bolts (Otto Wagner's post office) would be regarded as acceptable details of ornament.

Ornament, in other words, would be acceptable on aesthetic grounds as long as it did not function as ornament but instead appeared only as an elaboration of details and materials innate to the essential object of utility. Ornament's deviation

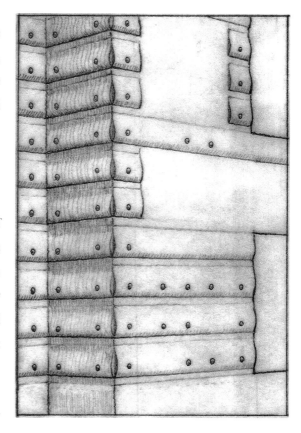

Bolts; Post Office Savings Bank, Otto Wagner.
Drawing by Kent Bloomer.

from this new regulation, its indictable crime, would reside in ornament's function to import, indeed to harbour figures that are extrinsic to the essential diagram and its tectonic minutiae, i.e. non-essential to pure architecture as defined by the revolutionary modernist ideology. Such imports are, simply stated, impure, unclean, and deviant when distributed into the fabric of modern architecture, and therefore should be forbidden.

Purity and its emblems of whiteness and cleanliness (sanitation) is an extreme condition because it conveys an abstract claim or wish for unblemished completeness. In design such purity is somewhat anorexic. An ideology grounded in the pure expression of building would consider the incorporation of an auxiliary like ornament, with the figures ornament negotiates to admit such as spirals with fantastic leafage, a contamination.

This impurity proposes a heterogeneity, a non-uniform condition containing multiple types of ingredients. Combining these different types may produce metamorphoses, e.g. figuration intrinsic to the utility morphing with figures which are obviously super-added and auxiliary. Such metamorphoses with their implication of one system undergoing transformation abound both in nature and in the history of architecture, and this intimate coincidence has often been brilliantly incorporated in the composition of buildings.

As an example, ornament's imported figuration, particularly in Western ornament, has usually appeared on thresholds and joints. Those liminal spaces, where the purely *utilitarian and diagrammatic imperatives of design are naturally exhausted*, welcome other species and activities. Ornament flourishes in the ambivalence between inside and outside and in the joints of structural transition (as in a column cap or zones of intersection between wall and ceiling). It occupies boundaries as it pries open their edges and thus "defines space and even creates such space that may be necessary to it".[xiv]

From the standpoint of perception such ambivalent figuration performing in the liminal space of utilitarian objects neither destroys the expression of the "diagram" nor negates an articulation of its fundamental tectonics. It is obvious that great ornament has flourished when (or after) the basic structure of its object is rendered explicit. Sullivan's architecture for example, like the architecture of the Parthenon and Chartres Cathedral, is muscular. The equipoise between ornament and construction even helps us see how buildings are organized and built as one agenda fuels the other.

Ornament, by its own rules, is a mediator and a collector of meaning from the world-at-large. It is a provider of intricacy. It can, at the same time, only be a detail. It performs as a messenger. It is an agent of design that thrives amongst differences and a visual power of resolution without a concrete formation until it is called into action. What, then, was accomplished by its removal from the discipline of architecture?

The accomplishment was to cement the credo of a revolutionary ideology proclaiming to be more modern and more progressive than an academic body resisting the formulaic destruction of traditional content. "Tradition" here refers to tracing a discipline (e.g. architecture, sculpture, geometry, ornament) back to its original elements, forms and functions, i.e. the ongoing historic process of the millennia.[xv] The replacement of ornament with a barren white wall was intended to produce a revolutionary emblem. The "whiteness", the anorexia, manifested the brave new project.

Fantastic Leafage by Kent Bloomer after William Morris.

would be no human mind, no education, no transmission of culture without mimesis".[xvi] In fact, both claimed to be carrying forward the essentials of great architecture. Even today, after the sacrifice of ornament, the alleged "modern", along with the traditional programme of study, still requires a certain amount of analysis of great seminal works. The modernists know they are beholden to them and unconsciously desire to be like them. How then did the modernist academy manage to implement the disappearance of ornament which was so visually prominent in the fabric of the masterworks?

The steps taken in the early twentieth century are remarkably similar to those considered by Girard in his discussion of the hostility generated by mimetic rivalry. Already the impulse 'to vanquish' was implicit in the battle of styles as well as an urge for a new style (or no style at all) capable of accommodating the enormous changes in building technology and building type brought on by industrialization and mass production.

In the early twentieth century the profusion and the confusion of tongues, particularly visible in the nineteenth-century panoply of ornament, provided an easy target for satirical and derogatory comments such as "deviant", "dishonest", and "non-essential". Thus the first step leading to ornament's condemnation was vilification and mockery. Girard points out that people and their progeny who exhibit extremes and are out of the ordinary, such as hunchbacks or kings, are the most vulnerable

Both revolutionary and traditional ideologies believed they could generate an architecture capable of contributing to the development of a better world. The modernists wanted to start anew while their adversaries desired to conserve attributes of the best accomplishments. Yet both unconsciously imitated the great works from history for "there and are selected for victimization in moments of conflict. Figures of ornament, viewed in this light, can readily be regarded as 'out-of-order' simply by recognizing their visual imperative which is to incorporate figuration originating *outside the order* of the basic utilitarian object. Ornament is meant to be a carrier and importer of super-additive and auxiliary content. That is its active cause. These adherent figures can be humorous; they are often metamorphoses and occasionally appear to be monsters, albeit usually playful monsters. Indeed Sullivan himself is occasionally referred to as the tattoo artist inferred in Adolf Loos's 1908 essay, "Ornament and Crime".[xvii]

Still, how did the spat exercised in the early twentieth-century schoolyard successfully lead to the actual elimination of ornament in the schoolroom considering that both the revolutionists and their rivals admired and were beholden to the great ornamented works from the millennium?

Triggered by catastrophic circumstances and the conflict climaxed by World War I, the subsequent need to rebuild provided a crisis of a magnitude that demanded explanation and resolution. The desire for a better world was intense and thus a second step in the playing out of a mimetic rivalry began to develop. To stake their claim, the modernists needed a victim, a scapegoat in order to inaugurate their official existence. They were starting anew and were searching for a rite-of-entry. Their scapegoat had to be exceptional,

a person or a personified condition of enormous stature by virtue of its pervasive presence, authority and historicity. Such a 'person' could be sacrificed and exhibited as a troublemaker. The act was to be witnessed by all parties. Indeed the ritual sacrifice of ornament would rid architecture of an obvious outsider capable of soiling and perverting their vision of a new and better world. By cleaning the slate a revolutionary order could be created and proclaimed by a ritual of expulsion, a death in the light of purification. It would appear to be an act of sanitation and would perform as a curative.

BAD MIMESIS

The execution took time and was assisted by a procedure that Girard refers to as "bad mimesis" as compared to acquisitive mimesis. Acquisitive mimesis means a strong desire to possess the object being imitated which, in examining a masterwork of architecture, must address the object in whole cloth. The "whole cloth" would necessarily include the ornament. By contrast, bad mimesis only allows a distorted act of mimesis. The modernists could enforce their special interest by altering the object of mimesis in a manner that might serve their programme of sanitation. They would obfuscate or denigrate the visible elements of ornament as unclean articles not to be seen or to be imitated even as they were conscious of their existence in the esteemed model. Such partial imitation, which re-writes history, is bad mimesis in which the 'self' of ornament becomes a 'non-person'.

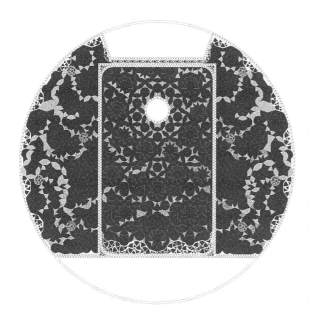

Symmetries. Drawing by Moises Berrun.

Controlled obfuscation is an instrument of "bad mimesis". We must ask, therefore, what elements of architecture are conventionally selected for analysis in our strictly modernist architecture schools today when great works are examined? What types of measurements are used in contemporary analysis, and how are the findings critically appraised and employed in the generation of ongoing projects in the studio or practice? Analysis is a difficult and specialized enterprise requiring a procedure of selecting agendas. For example one might emphasize the ordering of basic light, or the means of circulation, or the physics of construction. In visual analysis certain elements are often seen in isolation, apart from those excluded from the exercise. Thus it is within the arena of controlled, i.e. indexed selection that a particular ideology is able to intervene and diminish the import of its rivals. Valued attention is given to one thing

at the expense of another. Such intervention can substitute a credo for a reality, particularly for those who have not visited the actual works of architecture and for students who cannot easily escape a professor's procedure of limiting what is to be seen, such as tilting the image of the Carson Pirie Scott façade. Tilting the image was an overt act of misrepresentation masquerading as an act of scholarly observation. It was a lie.

Tilting the image produced "bad mimesis" by concealing Sullivan's actual ornament upon the building and by idolizing the reticulated white wall that was being foregrounded "with concepts such as originality and novelty constantly advocated [throughout the twentieth century] in an incantatory and empty fashion."[xviii] Sullivan's ornament is both a convenient and necessary element to be dismissed because it is so extraordinary, visible and astounding.

By ignoring and suppressing a quantitatively minor element, the impression can be given that "good mimesis" is at work. Yet, in the procedure of controlled analysis the visual state of affairs (the gestalt) can be entirely changed. The *pro forma* omission of ornament from an analytic format, if the omission is buried behind foregrounded images or within diagrams claiming to manifest progress, order, and innovation, lends the modernist project an amount of credibility by making it appear as though a precedent is being rigorously considered. Thus, while the mimetic mechanism may be unconsciously at work, the apparent mimetic content is falsified in the course of study. But is this process of "bad mimesis" a successful resolution to the mimetic rivalry between the proponents for and against ornament?

Viewing the architecture of the late-twentieth century (and much of today) we must grant that the strategy of eliminating opposing ornament has been overwhelmingly successful. But there are some intriguing fault lines in the means of achieving success that deserve attention in the light of mimetic rivalry.

In 1969, Alan Colquhoun, in his essay "Typology and Design Method", noted that the mid-twentieth-century modernists had been rigorously copying themselves [self-mimesis] for decades as they still largely do today.[xix] It is noteworthy that contemporary gyrations and formal wiggles have not really altered the canon barring ornament. Self-mimesis is indeed mimesis and it carries with it the rewards and perils of the mimetic process. Mimesis, whether it is of 'self' or 'other', fulfills both the necessity and the desire to imitate. "Mimetic desire is a form of aristocratic distinction, a kind of luxury…before modern times only the aristocrats could afford it."[xx] But can a routine mechanism of self-mimesis, if it perpetuates an emblem predicated upon newness such as the white wall barren of ornament, manage to survive today? Can its incantation and its repeated claim of being innovative and revolutionary withstand the monotony of reissuing the same emblems of inauguration for nearly a century? Colquhoun

revealed that the claim of novelty persisted while the implicit scorn of history (their own history) was overlooked. Meanwhile, the world around has changed rapidly and violently from the one in which modernism was born. Colquhoun was writing about modernist self-mimesis forty years ago. In the shadow of recent conflicts, will the activity of mimetic rivalry begin again, and if so will it include the proponents and opponents of ornament? Has ornament's status become so diminished that its importance will be overlooked once again?

CONCLUSION

Innovation is a valued response to conflicts and economic changes in the cultural, and natural environment. One of the transformative functions of ornament has always been to mediate with and to find the space for articulating forces, values and ideas that originate outside the tectonics of its objects, i.e. to locate us in the world-at-large. Modernism and its sanitized emblems of pure unsoiled space was, once-upon-a-time, stimulating, refreshing and appearing to resolve conflict. Can the authority of its negativism, however, renew itself after so many decades of its "bad" and self mimesis?

Perhaps the more important question might be, would the modernist project of architecture remain stable and culturally viable after a revelation that bad mimesis of architectural masterpieces from the millennium has been practised for decades in the

Academy? And what would be the reaction to finding that bad mimesis was the consequence of a scapegoat mechanism? Girard declares that the scapegoat mechanism, particularly the identity of the scapegoat as a scapegoat rather than a justly condemned offender, occurs unconsciously. (He prefers the term "*méconnaissance*.")[xxi] His theory allows that the omission of ornament is unlikely to be perceived as a cultural problem without an overt exposure of the scapegoat mechanism. However, such ignorance does not mean that the 'scapegoaters' themselves did not know what they were doing.

What then would be the consequence should the community, or perhaps more urgently the Academy, come to consciously recognize that the sacrifice of ornament was actually the "murder of an innocent victim"? What would be the reaction to the realization that the inclusion of ornament is, and could have continued to be, as modern as any single agenda valued by the modernists? "This would destroy the spiritual comfort, the righteous anger [the modernist believer] derives from the belief that [ornament] is guilty".[xxii]

i. Leon Battista Alberti, *On the Art of Building in Ten Books*, trans. Joseph Rykwert, Neil Leach, Robert Tavernor (Cambridge, Mass.: MIT Press, 1996), p.156.

ii. Christopher Dresser, *The Art of Decorative Design* (Watkins Glen, NY: American Life Foundation, 1977), p.1. (Originally published by Day and Son: London, 1862.)

iii. Kent C. Bloomer and Charles W. Moore, *Body, Memory, and Architecture* (New Haven: Yale University Press, 1977), p.17

iv. *Ibid.*, p.18

v. *Ibid.*, p.17

vi. Théophile Gautier, *Mademoiselle de Maupin* (New York: Modern Library, nd), p. xxv

vii. Walter Pater, *The Renaissance* (New York: Modern Library, nd), p. 111

viii. *Ibid.*, p. 114

ix. *Ibid.*, p. 59

x. *Ibid.*, p. 197

xi. *Ibid.*, p.199

xii. Kenneth Clark, "The Blot and the Diagram", *Art News*, December 1962): p. 31.

xiii. *Ibid.*, p.30.

xiv. Henri Focillon, *The Life of Forms in Art* (New York: Zone Books, 1992), p.65.

xv. *Edmund Husserl's 'Origin of Geometry': an Introduction* by Jacques Derrida (Lincoln: University of Nebraska, 1989): p.158.

xvi. René Girard, *Evolution and Conversion, Dialogues on the Origins of Culture* (London, Continuum, 2007), p.76.

xvii. Adolf Loos, *Ornament and Crime, Selected Essays* (Riverside, Calif., Ariadne, 1998).

xviii. Girard, *op. cit.*, p.77

xix. Alan Colquhoun, *Collected Essays in Architectural Criticism* (London, Black Dog, 2009

xx. Girard, *op. cit.*, p.75

xxi. *Ibid.*, p.87

xxii. *Ibid.*, p.22

WORLD CEILINGSCAPE

CULTURE·SCAPE

PRIVAT·SCAPE

CHURCH·SCAPE

OFFICE·SCAPE

FACTORYSCAPE

Dedicated to JAMES HILLMAN ~ LK 06

World ceiling-scape. Dedicated to James Hillman. Drawing by Léon Krier.

ROUNDTABLE

Excerpts from the panel discussion
moderated by Carroll William Westfall

Member of audience: I have a question. It's initially directed at Samir Younés. But to branch out to others. So you spoke of the mimetic rivalry and the dark tendencies associated with that that have pervaded critique of architecture and the relationship of architects to each other. So how or has the articulation of this phenomenon affected your own everyday existence as an architect? In other words, how do you mitigate it against these tendencies in your own life? And have you come up with tools to guard against it? And then have you and the department at Notre Dame been able to create some kind of structure relieving, that can short circuit these tendencies in the student dynamic? In other words, have you a cure?

Kent Bloomer: I was reading Girard where he said: as soon as the victim is recognized, and a real victim instead of a scapegoat, then the thing starts turning around. I mean, if the victim is a scapegoat and remains a scapegoat, then there's no problem.

Léon Krier: In order for it to work, the victim has to be innocent and consenting.

Samir Younés: Imitation is natural. One may say that is ontologically connected to the human character. It's how one learns. It's how one adapts. It's how one participates in and how one deals with society. And this concept has been under attack, especially since the late eighteenth century. The closer one gets to antiquity one finds imitative theory to dominate in general, although there are many dissenting voices. The closer one gets

to the present time, the exact opposite occurs. So that's an important point to call to mind. But the usefulness of imitation suffers when one's personal association with form becomes an amalgamation of the persona with the form. Many artists, architects, musicians, would have little ability to essentially disassociate themselves from that amalgamation. So, this is where the paradox is: the same concept of mimesis or imitation, is 1) at the basis of learning and the basis of participating in building a culture, and 2) also at the basis of conflicts and antagonism. And I differentiate between conflicts and antagonisms. In antagonism all becoming comes to a halt. In antagonism there's no becoming any more. It's either/or. Conflicts, however, can be amended. They can be changed and two conflicting positions, or more, might be perhaps brought to a kind of synthesis. So conflict doesn't negate synthesis.

As long as we desire form, and as long as there is mimetic desire for form – in the sense that we actually appropriate someone else's desire or someone else's work whom we consider as a model, a teacher – then there's always learning. We can always add to it, transform it. This is the useful aspect of tradition and imitation. It can be acquired, passed on, and through collective reasoning, when such a thing is possible, then one can build a rational tradition based on rational imitation. But something else occurs now. Now, that we've built a tradition by mimetically appropriating and adding on to other aspects of tradition. Now that we have identified our personalities with the forms that we made (you may ask: can one help that?) mimetic rivalry arises. Well, this is where the problem lies, where conflict and then antagonism arise. If one looks at one's artistic life, especially towards the end of one's life as an artist or architect, then one can find that there have been repeated attachments and then detachments from forms that one has cherished. But abandoning or destroying our idols is no simple matter precisely because many of us amalgamate our personae with our preferred forms. That is why many artists, many architects have difficulty in accepting criticism because the criticism – although they know it very well – maybe levelled at the building, at the painting, it comes to be necessarily understood as criticism of the persona of the maker.

Léon Krier: Well, I think really the lesson of... and that's why Girard is so important is that ...it's a technique. What he delivers is an instrument to understand the production of violence in any human compact, which he says and explains and is really understandable, why it's inevitable between any organized groups of human beings that rivalry is inevitable and it produces violence and it needs some form of management. And in old societies the scapegoating was the form of creating a guilt which would create peace instead of the vendetta which is ending by the destruction of the tribe where the rivalry occurs, and it's absolutely anti-utopian. And when you read that you wonder how anyone could ever have thought of human utopia because it's an absolute impossibility. The way we are created we are rivaling. It starts with your siblings and your parents and your family group and within society. And then you need forms to manage that violence. And not only manage it, become conscious of it, but reduce the amount of violence. Whereas, where we are now, I think, is that modernism is really a form

of exacerbating rivalry and is creating a scale of rivalry which is going to destroy the planet. I mean the planet doesn't give a damn about humanity but we will lose the very conditions allowing us to live together. And really classical architecture and classical building, traditional forms are known ways of how to create space which is humanely acceptable, where human rivalry of diverse scales can live together as neighbours, compete but without creating devastation, necessarily devastation around us. When reading Girard we realize that we live in a system which is irrevocably violent. And that our contemporary buildings and towns are an expression of a colossal, out of scale violence. And to maintain that out-of-scale-ness we need to subject other continents in bloody warfare. And because it's so awful and the guilt would be so terrible if we knew it, it is essential for us to delegate this violence and through mercenary armies so we don't have to deal with it morally. And those who come back who are shocked and awed to tears and to personal perdition, they get locked up in asylums and are relegated to finish their broken lives in slums. You don't talk to them, they lie on the way-side in downtown Chicago and New York. This is where modernist buildings can no longer be seen as an innocent game. If they have any value at all, traditional buildings allow ways to find back the human and humane scale.

That does not mean that we will all sing and dance and make love to each and everyone. We'll be as violent and inhumane as ever, but the means which we use will be less toxic and less self destructive. That is really the point of all of this.

Samir Younés: May I suggest one thing with which I was going to finish: that architecture is no more the property of a single architect than language is the property of a single poet.

Léon Krier: Exactly.

Samir Younés: So perhaps a lessening of antagonisms might be helped by further detachment from the forms that we hold very dear.

James Hillman: There's also a recapitulation of a very old theme that you brought up of a very old struggle which is iconoclasm and the violence that images release – thinking of David Freedberg's *The Power of Images*. And this suppression, not the violence, but the emotion, the desire, the passion, the eros that images release. And the iconoclastic tradition in our culture is so strong that it reappears, and reappears and reappears, and I think it's reappearing – in the way you've described architecture. And also the connection of ornament with "anima" (I would use the Jungian word), which is that aspect of the soul that I've been talking about, which has fantasy, has beauty in it … is concerned with those things, fantasy, beauty… not…I won't say passion necessarily but at least lovingness.

Kent Bloomer: Humour.

James Hillman: Humour. That whole part is … when I think of Richard Meier's formalism, you know, or Le Corbusier's, it's gone. And so where does it go? Where does anima find a place in the buildings, in the structures if we have simply heroic individual universal forms that can be put up anywhere.

Kent Bloomer: Ornament is extremely visual per square inch. It's one of the most visual things there is. Therefore, you don't need a lot of it to form the kind of iconoclasm. I just wanted to mention that.

Member of audience: How does one ensure that imitation does not lead to what is going on today?

Léon Krier: How does one avoid that imitation doesn't lead to exaggeration and that dangerous, toxic effect.

Kent Bloomer: How do you judge the right kind of imitation from the wrong kind?

Bill Westfall: I'll take a stab at it. If it's recognized that the purpose of imitation is to address the better qualities of people with whom you're living in a community, in a society, in a city, then you address the topic of your imitation to the common good, to that which is good for others, rather than to that which lets you stand out and apart from others. In other words, there has to be the brake that is provided on ego that comes from the understanding that you are fulfilled by your relationships with others. A building is a metaphor for this. It's good when it looks good among its neighbours and when its neighbours look good because of its presence. That's the same way in which we behave in society. There won't be that brake unless there's a strong sense that architecture is fundamentally a civic art rather than a fine art.

Léon Krier: You are really talking about the common good and what it is and means. Is it common to my family, to my peer group, to my class, my country, or the whole of mankind? The enormous danger that is developing is that the increasing rarity of petrochemical energies will lead to their appropriation by the most powerful countries to classes and people and the exclusion of all the others. What has already happened in the ex-Soviet Union where very few, a very small group of people are extremely rich and the rest of society is rotting away in pre-civilized conditions. So what can be done about this, particularly if we are concerned, as we are here, about building and architecture? It is very simple. We should plan and build as if 1) we didn't have slave labour, 2) we didn't have petro-chemical energies. Those two imperatives will not merely teach us where, when and how to build, but also how to make a better use of our fossil-fuel resources for the whole of humanity, not just for our family and our class and our colour. I don't see any means other than studying philosophy and old books about morality but they give little clues.

We don't understand the Qur'an, and yet it is an instrument that worked for a long time, or the Bible, but it's all terribly fraudulent nowadays the way these ideas are sold. We need something which is technical. How to operate in the world in a technical way which is morally responsible. And I think that the only thing about tradition now, which I think is interesting, is the technological aspect. How do you manage violence? How do manage building materials? Where do you take them from? What does it cost? Do you enslave people by having solar panels? Solar panels are, you know, seen as a common good – everybody should have them.

But without enslaving Africa we won't have solar panels. The materials which are within these panels are extremely costly and rare materials, and we steal them from Africa. And we subject those people to terrible conditions. So I think those are really the questions of building, urbanism, and organizing our environment. It's not about saving the planet. The planet doesn't give a damn about us. The thing is to get really very nice lives for everybody and it's possible. It has been for ages.

James Hillman: I want to say that tradition was emphasized. And there's one thing to be said about tradition that it in itself, although it can be misused as for slogans and for violence, generally speaking tradition has in itself a civilizing effect. Just in the connection with tradition and the awe that comes on a person in connection with it there is an archetype of the Senex, Saturnos, gravity that comes out of tradition and weighs and slows, and has a virtue of its own. That may be one of the civilizing influences that we're looking for.

NOTES ON THE CONTRIBUTORS

RENÉ GIRARD is a member of the French Academy and Professor Emeritus at Stanford University. He is a literary critic and philosopher whose work covers critical theory, anthropology and psychology. Based on theological texts, anthropological studies, and literary studies, his reflections on mimesis, mimetic desire, and mimetic rivalry have shown how mimesis, despite its fundamental role in learning is also at the basis of human conflicts. His discourse on the scapegoat mechanism has shown how sacrifice and violence have been not only at the origins of human culture but have also accompanied it throughout its history. Girard has taught at Indiana University, Bryn Mawr College, Johns Hopkins University, State University of New York at Buffalo, and Stanford University. Among his works (in English) are *Violence and the Sacred*; *To Double Business Bound: Essays on Literature, Mimesis and Anthropology*; *Things Hidden since the Foundation of the World*; *The Scapegoat*; *Violent Origins*; *Oedipus Unbound*; *Mimesis and Theory*.

The late JAMES HILLMAN was one of the originators of Archetypal Psychology. His imaginative psychology and archetypal psychology are a poetic basis for a psychology of psyche as "soul" restoring to psychology a fundamental element that it lost. Hillman was Director of the Carl Jung Institute in Zurich, co-founder of the Dallas Institute for the Humanities and Culture, and Editor of Spring Publications. He has held distinguished lectureships at the Universities of Yale, Princeton, Chicago, and Syracuse, and his books have been translated into some twenty languages. Hillman's *Re-visioning Psychology* was nominated for a Pulitzer Price. His intellectual roots include Renaissance Humanism, the early Greeks, existentialism and phenomenology. Hillman authored a number of seminal works including: *A Terrible Love of War; The Soul's Code; The Force of Character; Kinds of Power; Archetypal Psychology; City and Soul; Senex and Puer; Alchemical Psychology; Re-visioning Psychology; The Myth of Analysis*. Hillman has received many honours, including the Medal of the Presidency of the Italian Republic.

LÉON KRIER is a traditional architect, theorist, and educator. Among his most important projects are: The extension of the Lycée Classique in Echternach; Masterplan for Luxembourg; The school at Saint-Quentin-en-Yvelines; The Tegel competition; The Completion of Washington; Masterplan for Atlantis, Tenerife; Masterplan for Poundbury, Dorchester, England; his own house at Seaside, Florida; the Law Courts in Luxembourg, with Rob Krier; The Town Hall at Windsor, Florida. Krier is a fervent defender of the city and the countryside against their indiscriminate destruction through monofunctional zoning, and processes of technological development that have transformed architecture into a consumer commodity. As an architect who has provided rational strategies for the reconstruction of the city, and as one of the strongest opponents of modernism, his influence has extended widely into architectural practice and professional organizations such as the Congress for New Urbanism, as well as various schools of architecture, including the University of Notre Dame and the University of Miami. Among his publications special note should be made of his long-term association with Maurice Culot and the *Archives d'Architecture Moderne* as a forum of ideas dedicated to the reconstruction of the city. His book publications include: *Rational Architecture Rationale*; *Counterprojects*, with Maurice Culot; *Houses, Palaces, Cities*; *Léon Krier: Architecture and Urban Design, 1967-1992*; *Architecture: Choice or Fate*; and the *Architecture of Community*.

Krier has taught at the Architectural Association; The Royal College of Art, Princeton University; the University of Virginia where he was Jefferson Professor of Architecture; Yale University, where he is Davenport Professor. In 1985 he received the Thomas Jefferson Memorial Medal in Architecture; in 1987, the Chicago Award from the American Institute of Architects; and in 2003 the Driehaus Prize from the University of Notre Dame.

SAMIR YOUNÉS is a traditional architect, theorist, and educator. His writings focus on architectural theory, aesthetics, and the intersecting areas of the philosophy of history, cultural philosophy and politics. Younés taught architecture at the Catholic University of America, and since 1991, at the University of Notre Dame where he served as Director of Graduate Studies (1993-1999) and then Director of the Rome Studies Program (1999-2008). Younés is the author of *The True, the Fictive and the Real, Quatremère de Quincy's Historical Dictionary of Architecture* (1999) and *The Imperfect City: On Architectural Judgment* (2012). He has also edited a number of books, including *Ara Pacis Controprogetti /*

Counterprojects. Younés's projects and essays on architecture and aesthetics have appeared in international journals including *Architectural Design, The Journal of the Royal Institute of Philosophy, The Journal of Urban Design, Archi e Colonne International, Quadri e Sculture, American Arts Quarterly*. In 1993, Younés designed the monument for the Cornerstone laying ceremony for the Bicentennial of the U.S. Capitol, Washington, D.C.. In 1997, he was master-planner and senior tutor for The Prince of Wales's urban task force for Lebanon. His architectural projects have been exhibited at the Biennale di Venezia; The Gorcums Museum, in the Netherlands; San Giorgio Poggiale in Bologna, and other venues. Younés is a member of the editorial board of OPUS, a series of publications on the urban history of Rome.

KENT BLOOMER After studying physics and architecture at MIT, Mr. Bloomer received B.F.A. and M.F.A. degrees in sculpture at Yale. He was an instructor for five years at the Carnegie Institute of Technology and a frequent critic at the University of California at Los Angeles and the University of Texas at Austin. He has lectured internationally. His professional activities focus on sculpture and large-scale architectural ornament. His work is in the permanent collections of the Hirshhorn Museum in Washington, D.C., and the Yale University Art Gallery, as well as the Avery Architectural Archive at Columbia University. Major projects in public art and architectural ornament include the tree-domes for the New Orleans World Exposition, roof ornaments of the Harold Washington Library (Thomas Beeby, architect) in Chicago, a large tracery for the new Ronald Reagan Washington National Airport, which was designed by Cesar Pelli, and, most recently, the decorative frieze on the Public Library in Nashville, Tennessee, which was designed by Robert A.M. Stern Architects. In addition, he has designed light fixtures for Central Park and Eighth Avenue in New York City and for several university campuses. Mr. Bloomer's scholarly work includes the principal authorship, with Charles Moore, of *Body, Memory, and Architecture* and twenty-nine articles and contributing chapters in other books. His most recent book, *The Nature of Ornament*, was published in 2000.

CARROLL WILLIAM WESTFALL is an architectural historian, theorist, and educator. He received his undergraduate education at the University of California, Berkeley, and pursued his graduate education at Manchester and later at Columbia, where he studied with Rudolf Wittkower and Paul Oskar Kristeller, receiving his Ph.D in 1967. Westfall has held teaching positions at Amherst College; the University of Illinois at Chicago; and the University of Virginia, where he chaired the Division of Architectural History. Between 1998 and 2002, he held the post of Chairman of the School of Architecture at the University of Notre Dame. In 1974 he published a study regarding the early transformation of Rome into a Renaissance city: *In this Most Perfect Paradise, Alberti, Nicholas V and the Invention of Conscious Planning in Rome,* (*L'invenzione della città,* 1984). In 1991, in collaboration with Robert Van Pelt, he published *Architectural Principles in the Age of Historicism,* which brought together the poles of the current architectural debate. His essays have appeared in the *Journal of the Society of Architectural Historians, Journal of the History of Ideas, Journal of the Warburg and Courtauld Institutes, Architectural Design, Modulus, Threshold, The New City, The Classicist, The Encyclopaedia of Aesthetics, American Arts Quarterly.*

ACKNOWLEDGMENTS

Samir Younés

This book follows a conference entitled *Rivaling Desires, the Mimetic Psychology of Architects* held at the School of Architecture at the University of Notre Dame on the 31st of October, 2009. The participants were: architects and educators Léon Krier, Samir Younés, and Kent Bloomer, and the late psychologist James Hillman. Architectural historian Carroll William Westfall moderated the ensuing roundtable discussion. Many thanks are due to Michael Lykoudis, the Dean of the School of Architecture, for backing this initiative.

The editor wishes to gratefully recognize Mr. Jed Eide for his valuable support in making this publication possible. Special thanks are also due to Adam Heet and Thomas Sekula for their kind help in image formatting.

René Girard's "A Theory by which to work: The mimetic mechanism" is published with permission from Continuum International Publishing Group Ltd; and his "Innovation and repetition" is published with permission from the University of Wisconsin Press.